Pink Slip to POWERHOUSE

12 Steps to Next

Pamela R. H. Lue-Hing, BCC

Tracie,

Here's to Walking

in your

Purpose!

Abundant

Blessings

Always,

Pamela

2-24-15

Pink Slip to POWERHOUSE...12 Steps to Next

Copyright © 2014 by Pamela R. H. Lue-Hing

For more information, please contact Pamela R. H. Lue-Hing.

Phone: 800.975.9624

Connect at :

Email: pamela@pinksliptopowerhouse.com
Website : www.pinksliptopowerhouse.com
LinkedIn : www.linkedin.com/in/pamelaluehing
Facebook : www.facebook.com/pluehing
Twitter : @lpstrategist

Legacy Partners Publishing

ISBN: 978-0692238929
ISBN : 0692238921

Dedication

The keys to the rhythm of my heartbeat can be found in Allonte' Valentino and Carrington Marie: the two halves of my heart that make me whole. Thank you my anointed son and daughter for making me a better woman and a better person because of who you are: "fearfully and wonderfully made!"

In watching both of you grow, I have discovered more about myself and it has taken me to levels I never knew existed. Allonte, your entrance into this world helped to set my life on course and Carrington, you have helped to refine my direction. I thank God for blessing and entrusting me with two incredible gifts! Both of you are my inspiration!

To a woman who thought she could never have children; after ten years she beat all odds and bore a little girl. To a woman who dedicated and sacrificed herself to provide her one and only daughter with the best life she possibly could. To a woman who introduced her daughter to an amazing Lord and Saviour and taught her how to be a great mother, strong work ethic and independence. Mama, I dedicate this labor of love to you!

Daddy was taken from us far too soon but as I watched him journey to the hereafter; it gave me a reason to live beyond myself and the passion to serve others. I honor my father's memory with this work!

To my Lord and Saviour, Jesus Christ, I give thanks!
As I move on purpose according to Your Holy and
Divine Will, I praise and honor You Lord
for allowing me to be Your vessel!

I praise You, for I am fearfully and wonderfully made.
Wonderful are Your works, and my soul knows it very well.
Psalm 139:14
English Standard Version

Acknowledgements

Once I realized I had a voice, I knew I could not be silent. From the belly of Detroit, MI to the hills of North Carolina, my experience has been vast and intricately intertwined with many individuals who have impacted my life in such meaningful ways.

Bishop Desmond Tutu said it best, "To stand out in the crowd, only means you are standing on the shoulders of others." The shoulders on which I stand are vast and I want to thank everyone who has crossed my path and impacted my life.

I learned early on that people come into your life for a specific reason, season or a lifetime and wherever you entered, exited or remain, I am eternally grateful that our lives have intersected. Each interaction helped to weave a patch into my tapestry, my intricate being, and has allowed me to be exactly who I am today.

To all of my family and friends, I say "thank you!" Rita Gillespie, you always believe in me even when I waver and you keep it real. Quanda B. Anderson, you are the powerful wind beneath my wings. Liz Kimeria, my incredible Kenyan sister, you were the very first person to open my mind to the world of social media and I appreciate you.

Cousin Glen Hatcher and Connie Minnich, you both helped me in the beginning of this vision and your support has meant the world to me. Sharron Bowery, Chandra Oden Cline, Wilma B. Porter, Debra Crawford, and Rachel Orange, my long time friends and sisters, you always speak life into my dreams and I thank you. Carol Davis and Carmen Blackmon, your heaven sent prayers always give me refuge and the strength to carry on.

Aldreene Cooper, thank you for always being there and lending your honest feedback. Soror Tammi Hamilton, thank you for your creative genius and belief in me. Kenneth Morton, your words of wisdom, encouragement and spirit of excellence expand my capacity 212 degrees. Glenn Proctor, what's in a name? Only you know. Thank you for lending your expertise, editing my first chapter and stretching me. You raised the bar and were tough as nails but it worked. Theron Simpson, thank you for the inspiration, sharing your knowledge and being such a stellar individual and role model.

Denise Cooper, Raphael Love and my Millionaire Mastermind family, thank you for sharing your expertise and holding me accountable. Alicia Verdun, the masterful connector and my beautiful friend, thank you for always giving me your positive energy and sharing your incredible network and resources.

Thomas Co, thank you for your standard of excellence and challenging me to go deeper. Raphael Heaggans, your consistent encouragement has been refreshing. Elyshia Brooks, my angel, your tenacious focus and huge support kept me on task.

Commissioner Vilma D. Leake, thank you for acknowledging my gifts and positioning me to impact our community. Many lessons learned can now be shared with the world. YBM family, I am a better person because of your presence in my life. Arthur "Cousin Sonny" Symes, your amazing support has been invaluable.

Reverend Dr. Gregory K. Moss, Sr., my pastor and authentic inspiration, thank you for adding fullness to my wings. My siblings, Benjamin, Crystal and Felecia, each of you hold a special place in my heart. I will always treasure the tie that binds us together. It will never be broken!

Prelude

Have you ever said to yourself, "Today is the day?" But, somehow that day was not the day. In fact, it's been days, weeks, months or years since you made that statement. Well, today is the day for me. It has been almost four years of exclaiming to everyone who came within a few feet of me, "I'm in the process of writing a book." Exactly, what has taken me so long? Well, it's called life. However, I must say, since being given the vision to write this book, I have captured my thoughts and pearls along the way. The truth is "Everyone is gifted, but some people never open their package."

~ Wolfgang Riebe, 100 Quotes to Make You Think! ~

Today is the day I open my package and reveal it to the world. If you are in need of a gift that keeps on giving, this book is for you. As human beings, it is impossible not to experience or know someone who has had an encounter with one of the seven "D"s of life: Disability, Disease, Divorce, Death, Downsize, Disappointment or Decision. You are probably nodding your head because you or someone you know is facing a big "D" at this very moment.

The ultimate question is not, "Will it happen to me?" But, "What will I do as a result of it happening?" No matter which "D" has looked you square in the eye, there is something in these pages to give you hope.

After being downsized three times over the past 23 years, the huge waves came crashing in and the old adage hit me in the face at 100 mph, "Three strikes and you are out!" Instead of staying on the field, I chose to create my own game and design my own rules.   I became an entrepreneur. The truth is: I've had the entrepreneurial bug since I was a child.

If you have been met with a "Big D" in life, especially a "pink slip" and know you have a multitude of gifts waiting to be unwrapped, this book is for you. If you are currently employed, but have a passion, vision and desire beyond where you are, keep on reading. Finally, if you are an entrepreneur who feels like you are fighting an uphill battle, I encourage you not to put this book down.

In these pages, you will discover strategies you can implement, stories of tribulation and triumph to inspire you and words of wisdom to help you create your "next." The twelve strategies to move you from "Pink Slip to POWERHOUSE" await you inside!

Table of Contents

I've Lost My Job, Now What?

Step #1

Own Your Reality

"When God activated my gift and gave me freedom to flow,

He didn't just turn on a spigot, He ushered in a waterfall."

~Pamela R. H. Lue-Hing~

As we begin this journey together, do me a favor, take your left hand and hold it out in front of you. Now, take your right hand and pinch the back of your left hand and ask yourself, "Am I dreaming?" That's exactly where I was on Oct. 8, 2010 at approximately 8:45 a.m. I could not believe what was happening to me.

At 8:40 a.m., I held the position of Director of Community Relations at Montreat College and was prepared to give the weekly report to my boss. At 8:45 a.m., I was unemployed. He sat across from me and informed me that due to economic conditions, my position had been eliminated. Furthermore, I would receive severance, displacement consulting, and I had 45 minutes to gather my belongings and clear the premises.

I had just one question for him, "What about my staff?" He reassured me they were all keeping their positions. Forty-six minutes later, I stood in the parking lot next to my car and stared into the heavens. It almost felt like I was trapped between a dream and a nightmare. I had been released to pursue the next chapter of my life but the stability of a consistent paycheck and the comfort of benefits were snatched from me.

Just one hour prior, my mind was consumed with reaching an institution's goals, developing their plans and producing their workload. In the next hour, the calendar, project lists, follow up calls, hundreds of emails, goals, plans and workload were no longer my concern. By the way, my staff was downsized eight months later.

Three strikes and I was out in the parking lot, literally! This was the third and final time I would pour myself into someone else's dream. This was the third time I had been downsized. It was time for me to package my gifts and talents and pour into my own dreams.

Before I experienced my first layoff, I was very familiar with the impact of being downsized. However, I was even more familiar with the effect it had on families.

Daddy passed away when I was four years old. So growing up, I watched my single, determined and amazing mom with a high school diploma work hard as a cashier slinging chicken and canned goods on a conveyer belt. She worked for Chatham's Supermarket, a local grocery store in Detroit, Michigan for 18 years making $10 an hour. Her sacrifices and tireless work ethic managed to keep me in private schools and send me to college. Her intellectual prowess and money management skills could run circles around anyone on Wall Street.

This job was mama's solid rock and it provided security. She just knew our home was stable because she made a decent living and had good benefits. Prior to being a cashier, she made much less picking cotton and peanuts in the fields and red dirt of Tuscaloosa, Al and babysitting Mr. Charlie's little ones. When she moved to Detroit, Michigan she worked as a maid scrubbing floors and toilets on her knees at the Book Cadillac Hotel and served countless hours at the White Castle restaurant.

Eighteen years of her life were invested in that grocery store only to have her livelihood ripped from her in an instant. They went bankrupt. I watched her ride a rollercoaster filled with stress and fear of the unknown.

What was mama to do? She chose to reinvent herself. As we were going through this tumultuous time, I watched her chart a new course by pursuing her license in cosmetology. This new territory kept food on the table, a roof over our heads and the experience stirred up something inside of me.

After watching my mother work so hard and take charge of her life, the entrepreneurial bug stung me as well. At 9 or 10, I tried my hand at a neighborhood lemonade stand. Upon my eighth grade graduation, I had written in my journal, high school was a waste of time. I just had to hurry and college. I wanted to pursue my doctorate in psychology and return to my poverty-stricken neighborhood in order to open a community health and help center. By 15, I had started my own tutoring service in the neighborhood.

At 20, I began researching and developing a business plan for a hosiery apparel retail store in downtown Detroit called the Sock Shop. The legalities, licensure and feasibility study were underway, capital resources, equipment and the location were close to being identified, relationships were being built with wholesale suppliers and my mind was twirling with ideas.

I was so excited about the idea of starting my own business, but I didn't know how consuming it would be. I was employed full-time at a clothing store, approaching the finish line in college and found myself consumed with being an entrepreneur. The business was developing so quickly, I realized I would not finish school had I continued. Needless to say, I didn't pursue it.

During my short stint as a rising retail store owner, I learned a lot of valuable information. While researching and networking, I was introduced to Service Corps of Retired Executives (SCORE). This non-profit organization gave me a tremendous foundation of knowledge regarding business which would serve me well one day.

Two years after my college graduation, I found myself being chased by the entrepreneurial bug once again. This time, I turned my artistic gift into a hand-painted t-shirt design business and created unique fraternity and sorority paraphernalia and specialty items. Business was taking off!

However, it was tough being a one woman show. I quickly learned I simply could not be everything the business needed. So, I asked a dear friend with a finance background to be my chief financial officer. She agreed and we completed a partnership agreement. We were on our way.

Many opportunities came knocking and we were beyond excited. As we pursued retail licensure with fraternities and sororities, we found ourselves at a major trade show in Chicago. We took one of my signature designs with the intent of identifying a manufacturer who could mass produce it. The product was a big hit.

We knew we were on to something. This trip left us even more determined to keep moving forward. The orders were coming in and our calendars were filling up. All of a sudden, the partnership fell apart, the friendship slid into an abyss and we found ourselves in front of a judge. The business seemed to evaporate in thin air along with our friendship, something I will always regret.

Several years later, I was introduced to an opportunity that would greatly impact who I am today. I became an independent consultant and later a sales director for Mary Kay Cosmetics, Inc., one of the largest cosmetic companies in the world. It would take another book to share all of my knowledge, but suffice it to say, many valuable business lessons were learned with this incredible company. For over 19 years and three states, this company has been and continues to be a part of my life.

My involvement in Mary Kay Cosmetics, Inc. has taught me something that school could not: The art of transformational leadership. Transformational leadership does not mean just leading the way but empowering others to discover their own leadership abilities and use them to transform others.

The company taught me the principles of running a business but most of all how to bring out the best in others. I traveled around the country taking advantage of every training opportunity and learned techniques, systems, and skills from incredibly successful women. In almost 10 years as a director, I earned three free cars and had the privilege of developing hundreds of new consultants and future leaders.

Because of my life-changing experiences, my eyes have been trained to see beyond a blank canvas into a world of unlimited possibilities that create magnificent masterpieces. My mind has been trained to seize each moment!

Today, my children watch me like I watched my mother. As the world famous Les Brown says, "I am not just walking through the doors of opportunity, I am busting them wide open!" I am instilling the same principles, behaviors and attitudes in my children.

My 11-year old daughter is a competitive dancer. She is academically gifted, creative, thrives on understanding how things work and I am confident she will sit at the head of boardroom tables one day. She wants to be a chef, dancer and start her own jewelry and art business among many other things.

My 23-year old son graduated from college with his degree in Psychology and Business and he already has his barber's license with the State of North Carolina. He attended barber school while excelling as a student athlete in high school. The entrepreneurial spirit has become a driving force in his life as well. He wants to own a chain of barber shops, exclusive male grooming salons, and continue to mentor youth and serve in the community.

In between establishing his conglomerate of businesses and

utilizing his gifts and talents in the community, he is pursuing his passion of football and focused on getting drafted in the National Football League. He also has his eyes set on furthering his studies in sports psychology so he can work with young athletes. By God's grace, he will make it all happen. As my good friend Carolyn Walker once said, "A job is cool until you have a dream," might I add, "and create a legacy!"

As difficult as it may be, your first step must be to acknowledge where you are and the emotional pain transition brings especially when it is unexpected. Acknowledge that your life has been interrupted and everything has suddenly changed.

Take a few days to grieve, be angry, release the stress, and share your hurt or dismay with a coach, loved one or friend. Take time for you. After all, the majority of your waking hours were spent in that place. They saw more of you than your family and friends.

Of course you are disturbed, upset, frustrated, anxiety filled and a few other choice words. But you must force yourself to spend time reflecting on pivotal moments, then record or journal those past experiences along with best practices and lessons learned. Finally, release the negative energy. If not, it will become a ten ton anchor making it difficult for you to move forward and inevitability hold your visions and positive energy captive.

Now, you are ready to reposition yourself. Change is difficult for many people but it is vital to reprogram your mind by repositioning the known to make room for the unknown.

Your entire life and livelihood revolved around someone else's dream. It's time to prepare for your dream. After you own your reality, you will have freedom to flow.

~Reflections~

Step #2
Recognize Everything Happens for a Reason

There is a time for everything, and a season for every activity under heaven. ~Ecclesiastes 3:1~

Code blue, code blue, trauma team to Trauma Room 1! Ready or not, it was time to roll. My first day on the job at the number two trauma hospital in Detroit, Michigan and I was thrown into the frying pan.

My first case was researching and identifying the body of a young African American woman who had been hit by a bus. This young lady had no identification on her person. Furthermore, I had no training but I was expected to find this woman's family and contact them so the doctor could deliver the news.

They called us Patient Relations Representatives and we acted as liaisons between patients, hospital staff, families, and law enforcement. Initially, I was beyond thrilled to work in the emergency room and knew I could bring comfort to patients and support physicians and the staff.

No one could have told me I had enrolled in a crash course in medical school. From day one until the day I received the infamous call, there was never a dull moment. Have you ever had experiences and wonder where the pieces fit in your life's puzzle? Well, this was definitely one of those times. I was grateful for the increase in pay and benefits but what in the world was I doing in an emergency room plagued with sickness, violence and death?

Literally, I could write another book on my encounters with the heart-wrenching and life changing moments. When I began, my co-workers told me to be ready for the full moons. In the beginning, I didn't believe them. Low and behold, their words held true and every full moon I helped line up gurneys in the hallways and many times assisted physicians because we were short of staff. There was not an empty room or bed, especially, if you worked a 7 p.m. to 7 a.m. shift. Well, that was me, four days on and three days off. The worse cases were seen during those hours. It was never a dry moment and we were constantly in motion.

We had some mild moments when people just checked on the progress of their loved ones or when we provided resources for people in need. It was so fulfilling to hold the hand of an elderly patient who felt afraid and reassure them their family member was on the way. Many days my arms were wrapped tightly around that mother, father, daughter, son, child or friend who had just lost a loved one.

Then we had tons of full moon moments taken from scenes in a horror movie like the baby who was treated earlier during the day for respiratory issues, released and returned lifeless because of SIDS. This was a costly mistake that perhaps could have been avoided but the mother bathed the baby and forgot to put the monitor back on.

Many nights were spent in confidential briefings with police officers and detectives. One I remember like it was yesterday. It was an execution style murder that left two well-known brothers lying side by side in the trauma room riddled with bullet holes. For days, we did our best to stay on alert for retaliation while managing this family's crisis.

As if our work couldn't become more difficult, we faced yet another crisis within a crisis day in and day out. They were too numerous to count. It was the crisis of young, Black boys shooting each other. Many came in with their war wound stories bragging about how many times they had been shot. Other wounded young men came in talking and we just knew they would be fine but after surgery they never opened their eyes again.

Of course, all the cases didn't involve guns. There was the 23 year old who was brought in DOA (dead on arrival). While running from the police, this 300 pound man had a heart attack because he swallowed a bag of cocaine he was trying to conceal.

Males weren't the only ones plagued by the viciousness of the streets. We had countless females too. Did I mention the nightmares? As if the scenes couldn't be more intense, one night the trauma alarm sounded and we rushed to Trauma Room 2. The doctors, nurses, surgeons nor I could ever anticipate what we were about to see.

I held the door as the EMS drivers rolled in the gurney carrying an absolutely stunning young woman with long, wavy, black hair and exceptional gray eyes but a blood saturated body. How did I know the color of her eyes? Her pupils met mine in a fixed state as her lifeless body rolled pass. She, too, was DOA.

In these situations, the physicians would do an examination, record their findings and declare the time of death. As the doctor called out each wound, he measured the depth with his fingers. There was an eerie silence that fell over the room that night. First, he examined the front of her body and found a crack cocaine pipe in her hand. I had lost count of the number of wounds. Then, they flipped her bloodied body over only to find that she was being held together by the thin skin of her stomach.

The culprit: A machete. Immediately, I dismissed myself from that room and many staff followed. I had seen enough. There was not a dry eye in that place. Some met the midnight air with a cigarette, some of us wept uncontrollably but all of us were traumatized.

My son was just a baby. For months I had problems picking him up because I felt like I was touching that young woman's body. When I washed my face, I felt like I was washing with her blood. Many times I would awaken to screams only to discover it was me yelling. I knew something had to give. My heart had become so heavy and I knew I needed a change but doing what?

One morning, at approximately 6:30 a.m., just one hour before my shift was due to end, I was on the phone speaking to my mother with tears pouring down my face. I was having an extremely difficult time making it through each hour of my shift. All of a sudden, I was startled by the sound of screeching tires and a car door slamming right outside my office and the trauma door.

I opened the door to find a giant of a police officer running towards me with tears streaming down his face and holding an angelic 4-year old princess with long, dark beautiful braids in his arms. She had suffered a gun shot wound to the neck. She was gone. Her mother had been shot in the leg and was taken to a hospital down the street. As this precious baby slept in her bed, her life ended by the very person who helped to create her. It was her father who was also a police officer.

I was a part of an incredible team of chaplains and social workers. We brought order, support, resources and excellence within our scope of services. Indeed, we were the backbone of the emergency room. Physicians, patients, law enforcement, families and others depended on us. There was talk about a re-organization but we were confident they would certainly not disrupt the order we brought to the emergency room or so we thought.

It was 5:00 p.m. and I was preparing for my shift. I drug my emotionally wrecked body and mind out the bed to prepare for work. The phone rang and that was the call. It was my supervisor and she called to tell me the hospital decided to eliminate the entire department including her who had a master's degree in Social Work.

I was told I could come in and pick up my belongings within 24 hours but everyone had to be out after that time. A part of me leaped for joy, a part of me ached, and a part of me was left bewildered. I had enough of being a part of a thriller movie, I would miss our team and the light we brought into a world of darkness, but my livelihood had been stolen like a thief in the night. Strike #1.

Several years after moving to Charlotte, North Carolina, I landed a job as a recruiter at one of the largest woman-owned staffing agencies in the country. It was definitely a means to an end and I knew this was not my ultimate career because I felt a longing for more. I just could not rest and the thought of working in higher education began to wake me up in the morning and linger in my mind all day.

I began to research possible positions and submit my resume to several schools. There was a position at a college but I did not realize it was 90 miles away. I thought, "How could this be when I see this college off of the main highway all the time?" So, I continued to work as a recruiter and was able to help many find employment. I have learned that everything in life happens for a reason, especially if we walk in the direction in which we are being led.

In fact, I helped one of my best friends land a job at a university and she was able to get her MBA for free. Another individual in my family started with a company that I connected him with and it changed his life. Lastly, opportunities came across my desk that made me seriously consider working in higher education.

And so it began. Talk was in the air about a possible re-organization. We were a very small staff of three and we worked extremely well together. In spite of the uncertainty, we continued to work and wait. Then, without notice, the *big guy* came to visit us. We thought it was a meeting to share the restructuring of the company. Instead, he handed each of us the familiar "pink slip" and said it was effective immediately. After only three months of starting this new career, strike number two hit.

Now, I had to step up my process of finding a new job. I revisited the opportunity at the school and decided to walk my resume in the door. On this particular day, I drove until I found the school. When I arrived, it was almost like they had been awaiting my arrival. I was greeted with warmth, kindness, and professionalism. I thought, "This is definitely a place I can see myself working." After sitting down with the regional director, she confirmed that the position I sought was at their main campus 90 miles up the road.

However, after they reviewed my resume, she immediately asked if I had a moment. We sat down and to my amazement, she had two positions available at that location and I was qualified for both. However, my pharmaceutical sales and business experience made me a good fit for the development of their new nursing program. It was a mere concept on paper. She informed me when they started the interviewing process they would give me a call.

After five months of interviewing, waiting, praying and hoping, I was hired as the school's Business Development Specialist for the new nursing program. My boss who served as the vice president, was the best superior I ever had. No one could tell me that my position which I enjoyed so much would face such a radical transition.

One and a half years later, the school faced major changes. The boss whom I enjoyed working under decided to leave the college.

As if that weren't enough, the president of the college made a major announcement. In January of 2010, he notified everyone the college would be ending its fifteen year contract with a third party that was responsible for the school's marketing, recruitment and enrollment of the students. The most interesting aspect of this announcement; there was no transition plan in place.

When we received news of this change, I could not rest and the Lord moved me into action. I was led to create a new organizational structure and plan to replace the third party company and put my name in it as the director.

I presented the plan, made a few minor changes and it was accepted. For several months, we worked with an interim vice president and faced much uncertainty and unease. I worked countless hours developing a new department and hiring and training new staff while moving business forward, working with a limited budget and managing crisis simultaneously.

It had become like a scene from the busy streets of New York City: Calming disgruntled students, the challenges that came with establishing a new department with all new staff, tracking down misplaced financial aid awards and documents, rushing to fill cohorts starting in the next few days, broken systems, lost files and the list goes on.

We were in reactive mode and it felt as if we were on an Indy speedway driving 200 miles an hour with no end in sight. Everything was urgent and required immediate attention. I poured myself into this newly appointed position and many times worked 18-hour days only to have to pinch myself at 8:45 a.m. on Oct. 8, 2010. Sound familiar?

In a 26 month time span, I started a nursing advisory committee which along with the new nursing program director helped to launch the program. In addition, I was instructed to begin the process of starting a new Christian studies program, asked to co-lead a process streamlining task force and to be a part of a special task force to create a SWOT analysis of the impending transition.

Somewhere in the big blur, I also initiated a new committee and led the development of a process improvement plan which would have provided an effective infrastructure for the transition. At some point in all the chaos, the president selected me to serve on yet another task force and co-lead the new transition. Meanwhile, the new nursing program was being launched.

My greatest level of responsibility and adversity came when I had to recruit, train and manage an inexperienced but sharp staff while managing the crisis we were facing to keep the current programs moving forward and trying to launch the new nursing program. Not to mention identifying and learning a new technology system, advertising, and working with a company to create marketing collateral.

They say a boss can either make you or break you but have you ever had a boss you just didn't seem to connect with? Better yet, he or she chose not to connect with you and to achieve the goal by any means necessary. I may be far off base but the elimination of my position seemed to be part of the new boss's plan. He was hired five months after the major announcement. The irony: I was a part of the selection committee that brought him on board.

I always do my best to see the brighter side of any situation but have you ever felt your value was taken for granted? Well, this was one of those times for me.

Each day was filled with major miscommunication and departmental disconnects. I was in the middle of a crisis but remained a team player. When the new boss arrived, I even recommended one of my best administrators to him as an assistant and he accepted. Four short months later on October 8, 2010, strike number three landed me in the parking lot.

What was next? I was nervous about my future, filled with excitement about the possibilities, yet experiencing the emotional cycle of job loss. I began making a list of possibilities from next career opportunities, to organizations and community service. I read, indulged in personal development, ministry work, finalized personal matters, paid off some debt, explored educational opportunities, and applied for many jobs.

After meeting with the assigned outsource displacement counselor, all of her advice led to me starting my own business. However, she did not know I had already begun my research on becoming a coach and consultant.

I found my purpose in my past experiences. I pushed the rewind button, analyzed my entire life, careers and where I spent the majority of my time. It had become very clear I spent the majority of my time and intellect building and growing someone else's vision. But, I also uncovered my gift of strategic planning and my skill for business development. I had been released to do what I loved to do, serve others.

If those three strikes had not occurred, I probably never would have realized all the gifts and talents inside of me. Reliving my past experiences made me vulnerable but it was quite necessary to determine my next direction. Furthermore, I began to understand those experiences and the people I encountered were necessary to create the person I am today. I chose not to waddle in the puddle but dive into the ocean.

With each year the Lord blesses me with, I realize how interconnected people and situations are. Just think about the people who you have encountered along your life's journey. More than likely, you will agree people cross your path for a specific purpose which is either to serve you or be served. This even extends to the smile and greeting you gave to the woman on the elevator or the person who stopped to hold the door open for you. The smile you gave may have been the only smile the woman received all day and the person appeared just in time because your hands were full.

The next group of people appears during different chapters, seasons or specific times in your life. Perhaps it was your involvement with your child's PTA but now they are in college, the support group you joined to help with a life circumstance or the job that released you.

Finally, there are the people who comprise your inner circle and are there for a lifetime. These are your family members and best friends. No matter the encounter, each person has a purpose.

The second lesson I found to be true is people fall into one of three categories from birth to transition: Either they are currently facing a disruption in their lives, about to experience a disruption or have just overcome a disruption. You are no exception. If you are reading this book, chances are a disruption has left you at a crossroad. You are either facing this season in your life with expectations of overcoming or succumbing and can't see your way out. The choice is yours.

Many years ago, a wise woman working as a janitor shared a short prayer with me that sits on my desk today: "God grant me serenity to accept the things I cannot change, courage to change the things I can and the wisdom to know the difference." ~ American theologian Reinhold Niebuhr ~

This prayer alone puts the circumstance or situation into perspective and helps to release unwanted and heavy burdens because its foundation is faith, one of the toughest areas to exhibit discipline. "Now faith is being sure of what we hope for and certain of what we do not see." ~ Hebrew 11:1 NIV ~

Faith is absolute trust in God. It is like jumping off a cliff and knowing beyond a shadow of a doubt there's a safety net waiting to catch you. No matter how difficult, press on because it's just a matter of time before your breakthrough rescues you from the pit of uncertainty and darkness. Worry is a waste of energy and time.

Faith is taking action by acknowledging God has the master plan, the disturbance is temporary and everything will work out for your good. It's a mindset. The situation is preparing you for something far greater than you ever experienced. However, you must be determined that wherever God plants your feet, you will grow. Surely, He will show you one step at a time until you arrive at your destination.

Although it's challenging, why not embrace the process, operate in faith and expect a favorable outcome? Amazing things will happen and your faith muscles will be strengthened for the journey. Remember, everything does happen for a reason.

"Therefore, I tell you, do not worry about your life, what you will eat or drink, or about your body, what you will wear. Is not life more than food and the body more than clothes? Look at the birds of the air; they do not sow or reap or store away in barns, and yet your heavenly Father feeds them. Are you not much more valuable than they? Can any one of you by worrying add a single hour to your life?" ~ Matthew 6:25-27 NIV~

~Reflections~

Step #3

Define what your life means to you

"Everyone dies. Not everyone really lives"

~ William Wallace ~

From the very beginning of life, society's expectations are imposed. It has been engrained in the minds of many generations that college is the answer. Go to college, graduate and then pursue a career. Education definitely has its place but long gone are the days when a person spends 30 years with a company and retires.

As I raise my children, I am teaching them a slightly different standard from societal norms: Graduate from high school, go to and graduate from college, establish a career while developing additional streams of income, then get married and have a family. As a result, when the boss is ready to present termination notices or it's time to move on, a back up plan will already be in place.

I spend a tremendous amount of time working to challenge and train my children's eyes and their minds to see and think beyond what's actually in front of them. The bottom line is each of us was given a purpose and a choice on how we live our lives. Stephen Covey says, "Your life is not determined by your circumstances but by your decisions." It is not always easy, but what I have found to be true is this: When we swim in our purpose, our eyesight and mind become sensitized to the opportunities the human eye and mind alone cannot see or comprehend. It's as if each stroke you take, the sun shines on the water before you. That's if you are swimming, immersed and drenched in your God-given purpose. If you are not, the water is murky, the seaweed grabs hold of your legs and if you're not careful, you will find yourself drowning.

In either case, you must know the waves will get tough and the seas will roar but when you know Him and are living in your purpose, there is calm, a life raft, a boat, plane, or sun that appears in the midst of the storm.

Some fifteen years ago, I was celebrating my birthday in Negril, Jamaica. I was having a grand time lying on the beach and soaking up the sun. After hours of basking in the sun's rays, I decided to join a group of folks on the trampoline in the water. I thought to myself, it's not that far and it wasn't. The problem was I gave no consideration to the water through which I had to swim to get to my destination.

So, I jumped in enjoying my leisurely swim and all of a sudden the waves got bigger and bigger and mounted over my head. My heartbeat began pounding like drummers from an African village and a monstrous fear swept over me. I began to fight the waves but I was losing the battle. In seconds, I had swallowed an enormous amount of salty water and I remember thinking, "Lord, I cannot die on my birthday." The waves kept coming and in between the waves, I gasped for breath and called for help but I had drifted so far out, no one could hear my desperate plea for help.

Just when I was at my weakest and most vulnerable moment,

another mountainous wave shot over my head and through my burning eyes I saw a glorious sun shining so brightly that it immediately transitioned my thoughts from hopeless to hopeful. Immediately, I began to relax and become one with the waves. In between, I swam with all my might as if my life depended on it because it did.

This process continued until I finally reached the trampoline exhausted and feeling like a wet rag. Many valuable lessons came from this experience but two were very clear, my purpose had yet to be fulfilled and God is always there, especially when we need Him the most. The key is we must allow Him to be our guiding light.

As I travel this life, one thing I am highly confident in is that before the beginning of time, every human being was given a purpose. Indeed, it is up to you to decide your course and determine your channel. You can choose to wade in a small pond, float in a river or dive in an ocean.

Now is a good time to ask your self these questions: What does living mean to me? What does happiness mean to me? What am I willing to sacrifice? What are my non-negotiables? Non-negotiables can be defined as boundaries or parameters you set for yourself about what you will accept and what you won't. And finally what does my dash represent (the time between your birth and transition)?

Ideally, the dash should be defined by your purpose. I found the purpose of my life, the root of my happiness, and the development of my non-negotiables in past experiences. I am always enamored by people who overcome adversity and are determined to walk in their purpose. Thousands of those purpose-driven people have crossed my path and many of them are in my own family.

First, there's our family historian whom we affectionately call Cousin Sonny. Sonny has his doctorate in architecture, has taught at some of the finest institutions and is a thought leader in his profession. He is definitely a man of many talents. If you were to visit his home, you would find the works of his hands including furniture made of Honduras Rosewood.

Albeit, when Sonny assessed the dash in his life, he decided to swim in a different direction. At 66, he became a masterful sculptor. At 70, he became a professional model who graces magazines, billboards and commercials nationwide. Now at 78, you might find him centered in his favorite Tai-Chi position inhaling and exhaling, just taking it all in. But what makes him even more phenomenal is that he is a mentor to many and he has an incredible love for our family.

How about Cousin Thelma? She is one of the most humble and gracious people I know. In the Fall of 2013, Thelma competed in the World Master Games in Italy and Brazil. She earned gold medals in the 400, 800 and 1500 meter races. She has been a marathon runner for 30 years and even more spectacular, she has competed every year for the last 25 years.

Each year, she has been presented with gold medals in her age division. She has a bachelor's degree in psychology and a master's in special education. Thelma is 84 years young and she still enjoys working part-time in early intervention for the developmentally delayed. She enjoys tennis, theater and helping her community by engaging in local government initiatives.

2006 was a difficult year for our family. My 29 year old cousin died tragically and left three beautiful children. Shirley, his only sibling, had several children of her own and despite all odds, she along with her husband raised all seven children, earned her associates, bachelors and masters degrees all in a ten year span.

Cousin Glen grew up on the east side of Detroit, Michigan with his mom, dad, and siblings. After graduation, he enlisted into the Navy and became a Corpsman (medic). This experience inspired him to become a doctor of osteopathic medicine in ophthalmology.

He rose to the top of his field and is a sought after expert and mentors many doctors and those aspiring to become doctors. In later years, he found himself serving with the Flying Doctors of Mercy on medical missions in Mexico.

Now that he is semi-retired, he still finds time to use his training and expertise to serve along side a team of three doctors and a surgical nurse in an annual trip to Vietnam, the Philippines and Haiti. Eye care is not available in many of these places so the patients must travel great distances to seek care.

The team provides free eye care for the treatment of glaucoma, cataract surgeries, lid traumas and other concerns related to the eyes. They have seen as many as 1400 patients and 98 surgeries in a four day span.

Cousin Glen has been recognized with plaques and awards for his work in the Clark County School System in Las Vegas as he and his colleagues care for elementary school students by providing free eye examinations, glasses, and in some cases surgery for those who are unable to afford it. Indeed, he has found much fulfillment in his work.

Inspiration, motivation and knowledge were what thousands of people came for but my friend John Martin left with so much more. John, a program manager by profession, is the founder and CEO of an organization called YBM (Young Black Male Leadership Alliance).

Almost ten years ago, he attended one of the most well known motivational seminars in the country. As he was sitting there, he thought about how great it would be to create something like what he was experiencing but for young, black males.

In 2006, he began the organization and its' goal is to create a new reality for young, black males. The organization provides leadership development, college preparation and exposes high school students to professionals and opportunities they would not have otherwise.

In fact, my son is a product of this organization. He attended their very first conference in 2006 and there, he was inspired by a presenter who owned No Grease School of Tonsorial Arts along with his brother. Damian and Jermaine Johnson blessed my son and gave him an opportunity to attend the school while still in high school. As a result of their excellence and mentorship, the vision of becoming a barber, owning his own business and giving back to the community became part of my son's mission.

The organization also provided my son with incredible mentors who have elevated his thinking; hence, challenged him to grow. I serve as a part of the executive leadership team today to give back what was given to my son.

Under John's direction, our phenomenal YBM team has touched the lives of over 5,000 young men and their parents. What amazes me the most is John and his wife, Tammy, only have a daughter and no sons.

This final astounding example of living on purpose comes from one of China's Got Talent big winners, Liu Wei, a 23 year old pianist. The fact that Liu Wei was armless makes this story even more powerful. He lost both arms at 10 years of age due to an electrocution accident.

While growing up, he remembered being told by one of his piano teachers he "would never, ever succeed." Liu Wei's response: "For people like me, there were only two options: One was to abandon all dreams, which would lead to a quick, hopeless death. The other was to struggle without arms to live an outstanding life."

I have been blessed with a multitude of successful people who have crossed my path and are committed to making a difference in this world. One individual in particular who embodies the word "power-house," comes in the person of Dr. Gloria Mayfield Banks, an Elite

Executive National Sales Director with Mary Kay Cosmetics, Inc.

As a new consultant in 1993, I attended my first Mary Kay event and was mesmerized by this petite "ball of fire." Six years later she came to Milwaukee, Wisconsin to debut me as a new sales director. Later that year in Baltimore, Maryland, I remember sitting on the floor with a notebook and pen as Gloria poured in to me for hours. It was the meeting after the meeting that empowered me the most as her words satisfied my hunger for more knowledge and the secrets to her success. She was just an executive sales director.

At times, when challenges seem to overwhelm me, I think about Gloria. Like me, Gloria grew up in Detroit, Michigan. She had dyslexia but it did not prevent her from earning a college degree and a MBA from Harvard. After a stint with IBM and Stratus Computers, she went to work for Harvard with a black eye. She suffered from the trauma of domestic violence but she persevered in spite of the obstacles. While at Harvard, she began as a consultant with Mary Kay Cosmetics, Inc. and the rest is history. Gloria has appeared on CNN with Soledad O'Brien, CNBC with Donny Deutsch on "The Big Idea," ABC-TV and in Black Enterprise, Working Woman, Fortune and PINK Magazines.

Gloria has amassed millions of dollars in Mary Kay Cosmetics and her own company but what impresses me most is her ability to transform people. She captivates audiences all over the world with her amazing smile, high energy and ability to make you feel special even in a crowded room of thousands. Some of the greatest lessons I have learned on leadership, people and speaking, I learned from Gloria Mayfield Banks. She is a master at transformational leadership and bringing out the best in others.

Gloria, along with her national sales directors elevated my perspective on life and I will be forever grateful: my national, First Lady Crisette Ellis; Senior National Sales Director Kym Wells Walker, National Sales Directors Sabrina Goodwin-Monday, Nora Shariff, Natalie Privette, and Pamela Cheek. Gloria's friend, National Sales Director Nancy Moser also helped shape the person I am today. These women have earned millions in cash and prizes in Mary Kay Cosmetics, Inc., but most importantly, they continue to impact lives all over the world.

What I've learned from these individuals and so many others living a purpose-driven life is their lives or dashes are bigger than themselves. They take each day as an opportunity to explore a new gift, take on a new challenge, change or impact a life, and look adversity in the face with precise focus and sheer determination to keep on moving.

The truth of the matter is it's not about how or even when you die. Death happens sometimes slowly and sometimes quickly but when it does happen, it's final. Indeed, the length of life for everyone is uncertain. However, you have control over how you live your life and the choices you make.

Besides, isn't it amazing to think about the fact that a purpose had already been outlined for your life before you entered into this world? "For you created my inmost being; you knit me together in my mother's womb. I praise you because I am fearfully and wonderfully made; your works are wonderful, I know that full well. My frame was not hidden from you when I was made in the secret place. When I was woven together in the depths of the earth, your eyes saw my unformed body. All the days ordained for me were written in your book before one of them came to be." Psalm 139:13-16

If only it could be that easy to just follow the purpose and the plan. What happened between your travels through the birth canal and today? It is called life and decisions.

Exactly, what are some of those precious and proud moments that bring joy to your heart? On the other hand, if you had the opportunity to do it all over again, would you? If so, what would you do differently?

You may still be filled with anger and frustration about your circumstances but now is the time to push past the hurt and find comfort in knowing there's a plan and a purpose for your next chapter. This is the perfect time to call a meeting with your past and create a timeline of your life. Capture every significant date, timeframe, circumstance, relationship, jobs held, places and people served, and skills and lessons learned.

Do you recognize any recurring themes? As you thought about specific time periods, did your heart rate increase, perspiration unexpectedly seep through your pores, and a feeling of joy and contentment come over you? You may have even followed this feeling with the statement, "If I could do this for free, I would."

If this happens, you are getting closer to your purpose. It's like being in a dark room and all of a sudden, a stream of light peeks through. Inevitably, this purpose is bigger than you and it connects to others who need what you have to offer. This is also the time to keep your mind and ears open to opportunities around you. Be cautious about dismissing ideas without giving them full consideration.

If you already know your purpose, you are ahead of the game and there's true meaning in your dash. Your dash represents the life you live between your birth and transition. If you don't know, creating a timeline of your life will help in discovering the purpose in your dash and your existence will begin to take on a whole new meaning.

The search for your purpose can only be achieved in the dash. It is up to you to discover, embrace and walk in it. There is someone who needs your gift and is waiting just for you!

~Reflections~

Step #4
Challenge Your Fear to a Fight

What happens to a man is less significant

than what happens within him.

~ Louis L. Mann ~

Several months leading up to that moment, you heard rumors of a re-organization and pending layoffs but you thought to yourself, not me. Or perhaps it all came as a surprise.

One morning, you arose, rolled out of bed followed the same routine as normal and got in your car to travel the same route to work on the same job you've had for years. When you walked in the door, the atmosphere seemed a little different and rather strange. In spite of the thickness in the air, you walked to your desk and started your day.

Meanwhile, a part of your mind was consumed with things you could do nothing about at the moment, all the mounting bills that were waiting to be paid, all the needs of your family you simply could not meet because a lack of finances, and worse yet, you and the bill collectors were on a first name basis.

All of a sudden, the infamous "pink slip" was presented to you. It felt as if someone sucker punched you in the belly and caused you to take a deep breath.

Others of you may have risen up that corporate ladder and made a huge impact in your company. The boss sings your praises and shows his appreciation by giving you larger projects. You are proud of your work and accept challenges with determination and commitment. You work long hours and truly enjoy your job but you leave empty. You find yourself longing for fulfillment beyond the career and there's a void in your life but you just don't know how to fill it.

After working a 12 hour day, you get in your car, look in the rearview mirror and the person staring back at you grabs your breath and causes you to take a deep sigh. What's missing?

On the contrary, perhaps you struggle to get out of bed every morning and you awake with a "no, not today" attitude because you've got to report to the plantation. If you could walk away from this job you would, but you must put food on the table and maintain a roof over your and your family's heads. You meet your co-workers at the coffee machine every morning with the same empty, counter-productive "me too" conversation. You are restless, your mind is no longer challenged and the heaviness has begun to weigh on you.

As a matter of fact, the doctor just prescribed you blood pressure medication. This was added to your regimen of the anti-depressants you started taking six months earlier. In the middle of the night when your eyes close, it is then that your tears and your inner most fears meet in the pit of your stomach and the force of the impact takes your breath away. "You can close your eyes to what you do not want to see, but you can't close your heart to what you do not want to feel." ~ Johnny Depp ~

The feeling is deep and you can't seem to shake it. You feel as though there must be more to your life than this! When will the wind shift in your favor and calm your stormy seas? Something has to give but what and how?

Perhaps you are the person who has taken the bull by the horns and started your own business. You have invested time, energy, and money in writing a lengthy business plan, you have attended workshop after workshop, and every networking organization in the community has your email address.

As an entrepreneur, you may also struggle with balancing all of your roles: The C-Suites, president and chief executive officer, chief financial officer, chief operating officer, chief information and technology officer; manager, employee, secretary, human resources department, marketing and advertising director, the custodian and the list goes on. You work 12 to 18 hour days with no end in sight but this is a different 12 to 18 hours because it is for you.

Indeed, entrepreneurship empowers you but it does not prevent you from feeling alone and having little to no support. Quite frankly, many days you feel lost. How can you be more productive? How can you be more effective? How can you increase your revenue and profits? Maybe you are just starting out or you have been in the game for awhile but you work endless hours to find the answers to these questions, yet sighs fill the hunger pains in your stomach because you forget to take lunch.

Exactly how do you go from business plan to action plan? Exactly how do you manage all your roles? No matter which state you are in, from the person being downsized to the entrepreneur, it's emotional.

Experts contend there are seven emotional stages of loosing a job: Denial, disbelief, outward anger, inner self-criticism, withdrawal, reflection and acceptance. I must have been one of their test subjects especially on strike number three.

For me the "denial" phase began when the new boss was hired. Based on his interaction with me, I questioned my value to the institution and felt my time was coming to an end but I didn't know how much time I had remaining. Although I couldn't believe they would find no use for me, I dusted my resume off, began a slow job hunt and even considered going back to school. After all, my skill sets were used to lead those who held their doctorates so surely I was valuable to someone.

I may have been in denial but not for long as I quickly transitioned into disbelief. I simply could not believe the organization I helped stay afloat was removing me from the payroll. What? Certainly not me! Anger came over me like an uninvited guest and I didn't realize it had pulled up a chair to my table. The questionable emails, the infamous side meetings, and lack of critical communication played like a broken record in my head. I just couldn't seem to turn it off!

But, surely this new visitor couldn't stay long so just as the experts suggested, I performed a risky procedure on my brain, one that paralyzed me momentarily. I had begun the detrimental cycle of

"Inner Self-Criticism." My mind traveled back to the very day I started and I began to relive every single conversation I could recall, every assignment and every interaction. Was it something I said? I could've taken a different approach in that meeting? What should I have done differently on that initiative? Maybe I just wasn't good enough.

This self-inflicted torture held me hostage for a short while and the self-doubt caused me to "Withdraw." Quite frankly, I felt lost, afraid, devalued and all alone. As those four little eyes of my children looked at me as to say, "We are counting on you," I quickly had to refocus my mind so I began to "Reflect." This time, I forced myself to journey back down memory lane and listed every job I ever held, initiatives I began, and all the lives I had touched. My murky colored lenses seemed to clear and I finally "Accepted" the fact that I could not move forward looking backward. Most importantly, it refocused my mind on my God-given purpose.

As I reviewed my journey, it became evident that no one knew my true worth but me and God who created me. Some common themes began to appear like my strategic planning and business development skills, a passion for serving others, a gift of putting ideas into action, an ability to build relationships and connect people, and a gift for empowering people to discover the best in themselves.

After creating this list, I identified areas of improvement, decided what I would do to make a change and began to focus on it daily. Before I realized it, I embraced the fact that I was not in the middle of a nightmare and that particular chapter in my life simply had ended.

What would my next steps be? Based on the common themes, I gave birth to a new vision and signed up for a Christian coaching course. The displacement counselor affirmed me and I became even more confident in taking my skills and building my own company. The transition of my mind from employee to employer came easily because entrepreneurship is a part of my intricate fiber. For others, it may be more challenging depending on personal experiences. Either way, it is critical to understand the dynamics of entrepreneurship and its emotional cycle.

Whether you currently have an occupation and are pursuing a part-time business or you are embarking on the fearless journey of sole entrepreneurship, both can take you on a ride of a lifetime. I found it to be one of the most gratifying experiences in my life except for raising my children. It allows you an opportunity to discover new talents and skills you never knew existed and it can be one of the best personal development excursions you have ever taken.

Being an entrepreneur is not for the faint of heart and definitely not for the individual who only wants to work nine to five and get a steady paycheck. The good thing about getting a steady paycheck is that you know when to expect it. The challenge is you have absolutely no control over the raises and due to the uncertainty of the economy, you have a job in this moment but it could not be there in the next.

So now you have decided to stick your foot in the water to test entrepreneurship. What's going through your mind? You are probably experiencing excitement, fear, apprehension, or you just don't know where to start. You have a great idea but what's next? You have decided to dive head first in the ocean as an entrepreneur and ride the waves of exhilaration, anticipation, reservation and euphoria. These are all emotions that are bound to accompany you on your journey.

Your business is in motion but many days and nights you realize there's no one there to share ideas with and you are the only captain on the ship. The temperatures become a little too hot to handle. It is then you may experience a burst of cold temperatures and you begin to doubt your decision about going into business. Frustration sets in, you begin to question yourself, and glance back at the land. What was I thinking? Am I really good enough? Will they want what I have to offer?

However, you've drifted too far to turn back now and the determination to make your vision a reality gives you the additional energy you need to keep moving forward. After all, you may have invested too much time, money and resources not to.

Rest-assured, the emotional waves of entrepreneurship are many but one thing I do know is you get out what you put it in and you get to pick the ocean you want to swim in on your own terms. There's no better feeling. You have made up your mind, you are moving forward!

If fear knocks at your door or taps at your window, remember the words of Marriane Williamson, "Our deepest fear is not that we are inadequate. Our deepest fear is that we are powerful beyond measure. It is our light, not our darkness that most frightens us. We ask ourselves, who am I to be brilliant, gorgeous, talented, or fabulous? Actually, who are you not to be? You are a child of God. Your playing small does not serve the world. There is nothing enlightened about shrinking so that other people won't feel insecure around you. We are all meant to shine, as children do. We were born to make manifest the glory of God that is within us. It's not just in some of us; it's in everyone. And as we let our own light shine, we unconsciously give other people permission to do the same. As we are liberated from our own fear, our presence automatically liberates others."

~Reflections~

Transitioning from
Employee to Employer

Step #5

Make an Appointment with Yourself

If you can't see yourself from the inside, how can others

see you from the outside?

~Dr. Anthony Sanders~

Who would your friends say you are? Before you answer, confirm that these friends add value to your life. If not, you may want to remove them from the list of survey participants. "Never base your life decisions on advice from people who don't have to deal with the results." ~ Author unknown ~

Humans are a constant work in progress so you are not alone. Even though your neighbors Susie and John appear to have it all together, they don't. So be very cautious as you examine yourself more closely, protect your thoughts and do your best to refrain from comparing yourself to others. "Each one should test their own actions then they can take pride in themselves alone without comparing themselves to someone else. For each one should carry their own load." ~Galatians 6: 4-5~

Humans are ever changing and developing but know that each experience creates your now. If you don't already, begin to journal. It's as if something magical happens when the pen meets the paper and you capture those moments. After spending many years on personal development (and still do), this book was birthed through those experiences and the pages of my journal.

Your real work begins as you spend time dissecting the different parts of YOU from spiritual, emotional, psychological, physical, physiological and financial perspectives.

Each area plays a critical role in the life of an entrepreneur. Afterwards, you will explore who you are personally and professionally in order to determine your passion, capacity (how much can you take on) and your bandwidth (how far you can or have a desire to go). This is the time to define your core values.

Before a surgeon begins operating, he must scrub and prepare for the procedure. Likewise, you are entering the operating area. At this very moment, it's all about you. You must be totally transparent with yourself but patient because each area is a process.

If you wait for all the stars to align perfectly, you will never move but you will be much better prepared for the move if you are spiritually grounded. Owning your own business is a moment by moment journey and it's up to you to chart the course.

First of all, human beings are not just a living and breathing species. They have bodies that must be maintained and subjected to healthy conditions in order to thrive, cerebral matter that determines how they perform and function, communication skills that allow interaction with the world around them, and feelings. Lastly, they are spiritual beings led by a force much larger than themselves which is intricately intertwined into the core of their physical being.

It is utterly impossible to separate the man or woman from the Spirit. Many successful business owners I have spoken with shared that their spiritual life helps to balance their lives. One common denominator held true with these individuals, a personal relationship with God. Denominations were irrelevant and there was a keen sense of focus on the daily and consistent communication with God.

One of my favorite bible scholars, the late Rev. Reginald Moore, once gave an unforgettable sermon on "The Old Oak Tree." If my memory serves me correctly, his biblical text came from Matthew 7: 24-27 about building on a solid foundation. He told us a story about how he once experienced a vicious storm and the winds were blowing fiercely at what seemed to be 100 miles per hour. He was afraid but his curiosity got the best of him. So, he crawled to the window to witness clothes flying, trees being uprooted, cars being overturned and everything within sight was being thrown asunder. But, there was one thing that seemed odd to him. There was an old oak tree just bending with the wind and returning to its upright state, never be uprooted.

After the storm had subsided, his curiosity led him to study that old oak tree to determine why it had not been uprooted. He discovered the oak tree is one of the largest trees in the world and can live for 200 years. It begins as a small acorn. Once planted, its root system grows vertically in the earth for hundreds of miles even before any foliage breaks through the surface of the earth. Hence, it becomes an anchor for the tree. Even in times of drought, the roots can receive hydration from water in the depths of the earth because its roots are so deep.

Being spiritually grounded is like the old oak tree firmly

planted in the ground. No matter how bad storms get or the winds blow, you too, may bend with the wind but after the storm subsides, you will return to an upright state and carry on. Your faith will be your anchor and the Lord, your firm foundation.

On January 21, 2011, I wrote the following in my journal: "Today, I'm feeling truly overwhelmed and tired. I asked the Lord for strength because I feel weary so I opened my devotional. It spoke to all of my concerns. It's okay to be me today! Faith and fear cannot dwell in the same space." "For as he thinketh in his heart, so *is* he." ~Proverbs 23:7~

If you don't have a devotional, consider investing in one. In addition, it's vital to understand your spiritual gifts as you develop your relationship with God and seek to make an impact in this world.

Emotional and psychological stability is the key to making sound business decisions or any decision for that matter. Is your life in the best position to pursue a business or do you find yourself easily distracted by relationships or your circumstances and you just can't seem to get a grip on life? When unexpected events occur, do you fall apart? If you answered yes, in all honesty, now may not be the time. Perhaps it would be best to put a plan in place to better cope with your emotions and work through psychological issues before you start a business.

In order to operate your business and manage the multitude of tasks and people, it is going to require good health. It is extremely difficult to focus on developing or growing a business when you don't have the energy to accomplish the tasks or you are coping with ailments. Do you work out? When was the last time you visited the doctor for a check up? If you haven't in a while, now is the time. Good health is an important part of the equation.

Your perception is real to you and every decision you make is seen from that perspective. Hence, "You are confined only by the walls you build yourself." ~ Author unknown~

This is the time to demolish those walls so you can see what's behind them. Pull out your check book, place the bills and debt on the table and itemize each expense in your household. Next, itemize all income generating streams and how much comes into your home on a monthly basis. Review your savings account and assets. Ideally, experts say you should have enough savings to sustain you for at least six months to a year. If not, you might consider alternative ways to generate income. Based on your financial needs, do you need to seek full-time employment while you are building your business or will part-time suffice? Only you can decide.

On the other hand, perhaps you have been seeking employment and nothing seems to be happening. If this is the case, operation make-it-happen is in full effect. You have no option but to make your business work so be kind to yourself but stern enough to produce results. It is not impossible to build a business under these circumstances if you are determined and make the right decisions at the right time with the right people and the right resources.

However, you must also take into account your capacity and

bandwidth. Are you a risk taker and don't mind sacrificing for what you truly want? Or, are you conservative and cannot operate without a steady paycheck? Do you need capital to start your business or is it not necessary based on your type of business? If it is necessary, will your credit allow you to qualify for a loan or gain access to capital? Asking yourself these types of critical questions will help you determine your capacity and bandwidth in starting your new business.

Now is the time to issue a fair warning: Beware of self doubt during this process. After examining yourself, you may begin to minimize your gifts and talents or feel ill-equipped to handle the road ahead. Perhaps you feel like I did when I started this journey. I felt I needed more education to pursue my passion. Of course, personal and professional development is always a part of the course but it should not prohibit you from moving forward.

Case in point, when I was a twenty year old college student, I worked as a waitress for my cousin's company at an exclusive yacht club. While on duty, a wealthy, Jewish gentleman took the time to ask me about my life's goals. I told him I wanted to be a business owner but first I needed to pursue my MBA to learn about business. Emphatically, he told me, "You don't need a MBA to start a business." I just needed to start where I was and with what I had.

Well, he couldn't have been more correct. My cousin Judy who is like a sister to me finished high school at sixteen years of age. She worked for many years as a waitress. Her aspiration was to begin her own business by the age of 30.

By the time she was 30, she started her company in Detroit, Michigan with $600 on her Visa card. The company specialized in food service and facility management and provided staff for the food and hospitality industries, as well as, hospitals. I remember like yesterday helping her with the feasibility study and later being trained as her waitress.

Within 9 years, Judy expanded to Atlanta, Georgia and grew her dream into a 3 million dollar company. The client list included exclusive country clubs, yacht clubs, General Motors, Chrysler, Marriott and all major hotel chains, the Detroit Grand Prix, the 1996 Olympics and a multitude of other clients.

Judy's dreams, passion and strong work ethic landed her on the cover of the Wall Street Journal. Her company became a case study at the Darden Graduate School of Business at the University of Virginia. This young woman with a high school diploma and a few college courses under her belt started a company with $600 and was flown in to speak about her company with graduate students at a major university.

Twenty-six years later, she earned her bachelor's degree but it did not stop her from pursuing her dreams. As I have heard many times before, "Your gifts will make room for you!" You have three guarantees in life: You must pay taxes, death is inescapable, and you have everything you need to fulfill your purpose in this lifetime. "Our background and circumstances may influence who we are, but we are responsible for who we become." ~ Author unknown ~

Once you have assessed where you are and determined that entrepreneurship is for you, now it's time to understand one of your greatest tools: your personality. Your personality is the intricate part of your DNA which determines who you are and how you behave. Do you have a full understanding of your personality and how you can leverage it in life and your new business?

As a certified human behavior consultant, I find great value in DISC, the Four Temperament Model of Human Behavior. It was originated by Hippocrates, the father of modern medicine. The Model of Human Behavior explains why people do what they do. In his book, So, You're Unique! What's Your Point? Dr. Mels Carbonnel contends, "Everyone has a predictable pattern of behavior because of his or her specific personality. There are four basic personality types or temperaments that blend together to determine your unique personality."

Understanding DISC, the Four Temperament Model of Human Behavior is very simple. The "D" and "C" represent task-oriented people and the "I" and "S" represents people-oriented individuals. If you are a "D" personality, you tend to be direct, dominant, driven, determined, and a decision-maker. You believe in taking action. An "I" personality is an influencer, they inspire, thrive on interaction and are interested in people. You tend to make decisions quickly. The "S" personality specializes and is stable-minded, security-oriented, and generally more passive. The "C" personality is competent, cautious, compliant and contemplative which causes them to be slower in making decisions along with the "S" personality. Generally, people are a combination of personality types but one tends to be more prominent.

Dr. Carbonnel believes "How you manage your health, time and money are the direct result of how you govern your personality. Identifying and understanding your temperament and motivations can make the difference between your success or failure, especially as a leader and business person."

Now that you understand a little bit about personality types, what are your gifts and talents? Most people are clear about their gifts and talents but are unclear about how to use them. For those who are clear in both areas, this next exercise may be helpful in uncovering other gifts as well.

When I was downsized for the third time, I took some time to do something I had never done before and it brought clarity regarding my strengths. I created a timeline of my life. As I made each entry, I included specific jobs I held, ministry and volunteer work, hobbies explored, clubs and organizations to which I had belonged, net-working events I had attended throughout the years, personal and professional development engagement, workshops and educational advancement opportunities, and lastly a long list of potential income producing ideas which I had once participated in or were currently considering. I also took some time to update my resume. This activity alone helped to boost my confidence in my abilities and recognize my skill sets.

When creating a timeline and taking an inventory of your gifts and talents, make sure you identify common themes and patterns in your life. Also give much thought to your work ethic. This will give you more insight about your capacity and bandwidth as you move forward to start and grow a business.

After creating my timeline, I became crystal clear on my next chapter and my new business began to unfold. More importantly, the mission for my life was defined: To be a change agent wherever I am planted, inspire those to whom I have been assigned to maximize their God-given gifts and talents for His Glory and to make a positive impact in the lives of others.

If the exercises in this chapter are done thoroughly, your passions will have emerged and your legacy will take root to impact future generations. Passion is love on fire. "Love recognizes no barriers. It jumps hurdles, leaps fences, penetrates walls to arrive at its destination full of hope." ~ Maya Angelou ~

Discovering your passion is essential to this step and belief in yourself is a paramount principle of life. "Belief is trust, faith, or confidence in someone or something." Ultimately, you will become what you believe about yourself.

"There's an old story about a farmer who found an eagle's egg and not knowing what else to do, he put it in the nest of a backyard chicken. The egg hatched and the eaglet grew up with the brood of chicks.

It was only natural that the eagle should do what the backyard chickens did, as he just assumed he was a backyard chicken, too. He scratched the ground for worms and insects; clucked and cackled; and sometimes even would thrash his wings and fly a few feet in the air. Year after year, it was the same thing.

After years had passed, and he was old, he saw a magnificent bird soaring far above the farmyard. It seemed like it was enjoying gracefully gliding among the powerful wind currents, with very little movement of the wings.

The old eagle looked up and asked, "Who's that?" His neighbor said, "That's the eagle, the grandest of birds. He belongs to the sky, while we belong to the earth for we are chickens." So the eagle lived and died a chicken, for that's what he thought he was." This story epitomizes a quote by Henry Ford, "You are what you think you are. Whether you think you can or can't, you're right."

~Reflections~

Step #6
Create Your Success Team

"Teamwork: It is a fact that in the right formation, the lifting power of many wings can achieve twice the distance of any bird flying alone." ~ Author Unknown~

Throughout my life, I have been intrigued by the lives of successful people. These people influence and challenge your thinking which keeps you on the right track. As I examined the lives of these people and in particular, people in business, I found two common themes: Mindset and the fact they all have what I refer to as a "Success Team."

"Success Team" is comprised of a formula I created which combines the engagement of people and contributing factors that support the accomplishment of a goal or objective. It is an acronym that represents: People, Behaviors, Attitudes, Organizations, Things and Circumstances or PBAOTC (pronounced Pa-Bot-See).

In this chapter you will gain greater insight about each area in the formula. This formula can be used as a tool to build and grow your business. More importantly, it provides an opportunity to take an in-depth look at where you are in each area. It will either affirm you are headed in the right direction or give you insight on setting a new course. As a result of working through this formula, you can develop a solid "Success Team" that will not only help you grow your business but impact your entire life.

Whenever I encounter a successful person, it's as if school is in session for me. My antennas go up, I grab my pen and paper, and the questions begin.

I will share insights from several successful people in my inner circle who have together amassed over 75 years of being in business for themselves. Their expertise is diverse and their insights are timely.

Liz Kimeria runs her own business remotely. When this former top sales director in Mary Kay decided to do something different with her career, she taught herself the world of social media and how to build blogs and websites. This stay at home mom has built an incredibly successful business that teaches people how to do the same. She has clientele all over the world.

Rita Gillespie once worked in accounting but the company filed bankruptcy and she received a "pink slip." She wandered aimlessly for six months and had no clue about her next career. But she was determined to never let anyone "define her" and have that much control over her life and her family. She realized she had a passion for serving others and started a childcare business. She owned the business for ten years and has owned and operated a group home for almost eight years.

The real estate market has always been a profitable industry until its decline in recent years. But, Rodney Jackson has stood the test of time with over thirty years in residential real estate. He receives referrals consistently from lenders, other agents, past clients and attorneys who value his expertise and is known for producing results and satisfied clients.

These are people who at one time, worked for someone else but decided to take their gifts, passions, and purposes and create their own legacies. You will get a glimpse into how they think, run their businesses and how each area of the Success Team formula impacts them in the Pearls of Wisdom.

<u>People</u>

Let's begin by addressing the people or better yet, the power of influences in your life. Have you heard the saying, "You become like the people you hang around or surround yourself with?" These people can be defined as your inner circle. People can be a rock on which you stand or they can become the rock that takes you under. "As iron sharpens iron, so one man sharpens another." ~ Proverbs 27:17 NIV ~

Inner circles influence thought, positively or negatively. Do the people who are closest to you support your dreams and aspirations or do they come with a gallon of water ready to put your fire out? If selected carefully, inner circles move you into action, take you to the next level, and hold you accountable as you take flight.

Successful people have inner circles in every area of their lives personally, professionally, spiritually, physically, psychologically, and intellectually. Many things you do not have control over but creating your circle of influence is critical and definitely one area in which you have total control.

When you have the support you need, you will experience a healthy balance of working on your business, as well as, in your business. Michael E. Gerber, author of The E-Myth Revisited: Why Most Small Businesses Don't Work and What to Do About It, does an excellent job of describing three important roles as an entrepreneur: The Visionary, the Manager and the Technician. He explains how entrepreneurs are great at working in their passion or gift but don't know how to run a business effectively. Having the right people and resources in place will help you balance your roles.

Every great athlete is surrounded by a team of advisors and coaches. If you are in business, consider yourself an athlete because every day is your training ground and you are constantly faced with competition and adversity.

Develop a relationship with an industry specific mentor or someone you can trust who can help chart your course. Assemble a sound team of experts comprised of (at least) a business advisor/ strategist/coach; attorney; accountant/ bookkeeper; branding and marketing professional; and social media expert. Mastermind groups can be extremely beneficial as well. Take an honest look at the people in your life and make a decision.

~Inner Circle Pearls of Wisdom on People~

"I learn from the people I work with and seek people who have like mindsets. I identify target markets and build strong

relationships with people who align with my passion and who need what I have to offer. I know what my customers want. " ~ **Liz** ~

"I am very compassionate so I must be careful how I separate my compassion from my business. " ~ **Rita**~

"I align myself with people who are headed or currently in the direction I want to go such as being successful in their marriages, those who have spiritual peace and doing their own business. I spend time with those who bring knowledge and laughter to my life and those with whom I can share ideas and are focused and full of joy." ~ **Rodney**~

Behavior & Attitude

Someone once said, "You can't stop people from being who they are, but you can stop YOU from being who you are not." Who are you to be? It is a fact, that Behavior and Attitude are interdependent. One can't exist without the other. Webster's dictionary defines **Behavior** as "the manner of one's conduct or any observable response of an organism to stimuli;" and **Attitude** as "a state of mind, behavior, or conduct, as indicating one's feelings, opinion, or purpose." Based on these definitions, it is safe to say that attitude is reflected in and affects behavior.

Who are you to be? Every successful person I have read about, heard about or spoken to has amazing attitudes and consistent and productive behaviors. These are great attributes that lead to outstanding character.

How do you face each day? The alarm clock goes off and

your eyes open. Do you rise with excitement and anticipation? Do you spend time with your Creator thanking Him for another day of opportunity and asking Him to order your steps for the day? Do you spend quiet time meditating and reflecting before the gun goes off to begin your marathon?

On the other hand, do you hit the alarm clock dreading the day's schedule? Do you awaken to the infamous doldrums "the dumps?" You know the one that causes you to think "I wish I had a sludge hammer…no, not again…give me thirty more minutes." If this is the case, chances are you must definitely evaluate your behaviors and attitudes. "When you change the way you look at things, the things you look at begin to change" ~ Anonymous~

As hard as we may try, we simply can not separate personal from business. Ultimately, the business reflects the person. The way we act and how we operate in our personal life is intimately connected with all areas. In fact, each area takes on a life of itself and is either thriving or suffering from malnutrition. How are you feeding each area?

~Inner Circle Pearls of Wisdom on Behaviors & Attitudes~

"My work ethic is strong and my mindset is not a 9-5 mindset. I am clear on the attitudes I exhibit. I discipline myself by having a consistent daily schedule. I am extremely focused and work on one project at a time until it is finished. My mindset is my greatest asset and I have a strong belief in my vision. As long as I can see it, I can

do it!" ~ Liz ~

"I am a workaholic but I absolutely love what I do. I am kind and considerate of others. I have been told I have a loving attitude and I refrain from being judgmental. Although I delegate, I don't believe anyone can do it better than me because it's my vision, so of course they wouldn't but I do allow them freedom to carry out the task in their own unique way. I keep a positive attitude and my faith and trust in God helps me. As a business owner, sometimes I can't see the forest for the trees but I learn from past mistakes. I take my blinders off, accept the ugly with the good, take ownership, and seek help. I used to wear my emotions on my sleeves but now I ask myself 'what's best for the business,' and make sure my strategic plan is aligned with my goals especially financially"~ Rita ~

"I am true to myself. I am persistent, consistent, and laser focused. I have noticed when I lose focus, I lose business. The lesson I learned is this journey is a faith walk and I must exercise it because being a business owner takes all of it. I love the adventure and I don't see owning a business as a job but I don't live for business, it's something I love to do. I work from my passion. I am teachable and I tell myself 'I know how to do this.' I share more with people who are serious, my mind must constantly be in the right place and I must have balance." ~ Rodney ~

Organization(s)

In this section, I want to challenge you to evaluate how you organize yourself daily for success. In addition, we want to also take an in-depth look of the organizations to which you belong. The ultimate goals are to create strong *organizational systems* and to align yourself or business with *organizations* that help you accomplish your vision and mission.

I have attended hundreds of workshops, seminars, conferences, and symposiums over the years featuring "successful people." If there is one consistent message regarding organization, it would be each person created a system. After creating systems, their next challenge was allowing the systems to guide their daily tasks and workload.

As it relates to organizations, it is essential to your business or goal that you align yourself with the right organizations. Organizations are where relationships are formed. Every organization has a defined purpose and with every purpose comes an opportunity to give of your talents and skills and build your business.

Professionally, organizations provide education, create strategic alliances, partnerships, collaborations, mastermind groups, and the list goes on. Organizations are a critical component of professional development and success in moving business and/or careers forward but the investment of time and money must be taken into account. It is most effective when the organization is aligned with your goals and mission.

If an organization does not exist to suit your needs, create one because it is vital to keeping your pipeline filled with potential clients and opportunities.

It is also equally important to your growth as a person and to the community to identify organizations to which you can volunteer. Human beings need organizations and organizations need human beings. They help a person grow in so many different ways. As a child, the core value of citizenship is instilled. We are taught to make positive contributions in our communities or society and to have a servant's attitude.

The vitality and value of your Success Team strongly depend on your ability to organize yourself and align yourself with the right organizations strategically!

~Inner Circle Pearls of Wisdom on Organization(s) ~

"I position myself to always learn from others. I write projects down and work on it until the project is complete. I check emails later in the day unless something requires my urgent attention and I found writing the six most important tasks for the day is very helpful." ~Liz ~

"My business must have structure. In order to maximize my time, I take a notebook and write everything down then prioritize them." ~ Rita ~

"I allocate my time wisely and build in personal time. Daily reminders of important tasks are integrated in my day because I must see it. I found associations and boards help build relationships. Over the years, I have learned to balance my business with family, spiritual life and friends. Business is just something I do and my life must be balanced. I create systems that create business and my follow up is

*key. I have a coach because I realize I can't do it on my own. I organize my daily activities to get everything done and when I do it creates a great sense of satisfaction and feeling of success. I keep an appointment with myself to workout 5-6 days per week and volunteer at church and with other service-oriented activities. Organizations must be industry specific and fit where I am going." ~ **Rodney** ~*

Things

The word "Thing" has many definitions. However, we will focus on "Thing" as defined in Webster's Dictionary as "that which is designated." So, exactly what types of "Things" or activities can you add or designate to your Success Team?

For starters, as we move well into the 21st Century, technology is at the tip of our fingers, literally. Everything around us operates via technology including many of our schedules. For most people, when their technology is inoperable, so are they. Some will say that the old method of capturing thoughts and ideas is antiquated but I contend there is still power in the pen and power in the paper.

Journaling is an extremely powerful tool and has become an essential part of my life. It helps reflect, stay on track and keep creative juices flowing. It doesn't matter where you are, it works when you use it whether you are reflecting on your day, expressing gratitude, defining your next chapter in life, writing a book, or creating a new business. A journal can be one of your best allies. It is critical to set aside the time each day for this activity. If you have not tried it before, it may take some time to discipline yourself but the most important key is to just get started.

A person who reads is a person who is open to receiving. Reading energizes your creative process, unlocks your understanding and propels you forward. As the chief executive officer of your company, it's imperative to stay abreast of industry standards, products, services, competition, most of all your professional development.

Another "Thing" I found essential to having a productive day is making a short list of key projects and tasks before I begin each day. This helps with focus and gives a sense of accomplishment once the task is complete. Using Sunday evening to plan creates an even more productive and powerful week! Beginning the day with reading the Bible, devotionals and prayer are other ways to become centered and move in the right directions.

Several "Things" or exercises I found to be extremely empowering, I learned from my mentor and multi-millionaire, Dr. Gloria Mayfield Banks. She taught me to create a list of at least 50 things I want to do or have happen as a result of achieving certain levels in my life. She also introduced me to the concept of creating a dream book. These exercises will help with focus and to engage your family in your goals.

It's up to you to define the "Things" you need in order to help you be productive and once identified, the key will be consistency and there will be a need to evaluate effectiveness periodically.

~Inner Circle Pearls of Wisdom on Things~

"I take time to meditate each day and find quiet time to read books for personal growth." ~**Liz** ~

"I watch my money daily and review emails in the morning. I created systems for all of my paperwork and set daily agendas. I know my rhythm, get the proper rest; and make sure I have my spiritual time to allow my faith to grow." ~ **Rita** ~

"I focus on my marketing and prospecting daily. My philosophy is ready, fire then aim. This has led to creating tremendous opportunities because I try things outside the box that I would have procrastinated about. I focus my mind daily in order to decide where I want to go and how I want to increase my business. I am forward thinking and I make my wife who is also my business partner, a part of what I do and we take time together." ~ **Rodney** ~

Circumstances

Now that you have spent time analyzing the People, Behaviors, Attitudes, Organizations, and Things, let's take a look at "Circumstances." A Spanish philosopher, George Santayana, wrote in his Reason in Common Sense, The Life of Reason, Volume 1, "Those who cannot remember the past are condemned to repeat it." However, the Success Team formula is designed to keep you focused on moving forward. So, let's choose to focus on the adage, "It is not about what happens to you in your life but how you choose to respond."

In 2011, seven professional athletes were inducted in the NFL

Hall of Fame. What stood out most was the defining moments in their lives that helped create their drive and determination to succeed.

For instance, Deion Sanders, one of the most charismatic players to ever grace a NFL football field shared a story about his mom for the first time. He gave his mom all the credit but he had not always acknowledged her as a driving force. In fact, growing up, he admitted he was ashamed of her. His mom worked as a custodian in a hospital to provide for their family and to afford him an opportunity to play football.

One day, one of Deion's friends was at the hospital where his mom worked. His friend saw his mother working and later told him. He was ashamed to admit he was embarrassed.

Later, he vowed to be successful so his mom would never have to work another day. And so it is.

The circumstances in my life that drive me like none other are providing the best life for my children and caring for all of the needs of my seasoned mother.

As a single parent, I watched my mother sacrifice to send me to private schools and college. I watched fear consume her head as that job she counted on day in and day out was snatched from her when the company went bankrupt. My goal is to make her extremely comfortable and give my children even more opportunities than I had.

Secondarily, after being downsized three times in my life and watching my mother endure the stormy seas, I help others who have been, are currently in or will be facing the same disturbances my mother and I both experienced. This has driven me to create my company and help people all around the world develop their gifts and talents to serve others through entrepreneurship.

A radio personality said, "Perspective influences position and choices." What is your perspective about your circumstances? Have you taken the time to sharpen your vision to see the opportunities in all circumstances? Today is the day to take flight and use your circumstances as a launching pad!

~Inner Circle Pearls of Wisdom on Circumstances~

*"When I go through a crisis I must continue work. If I don't, two crises will be created: The one I am in and the one that will be created because I didn't continue to work. I always think, 'How will I come through on the other side and what's going to be the outcome?' Another life depends on me and failure is not an option." ~ **Liz** ~*

"Knowing people depend on me is what drives me. I've learned success is much bigger than the person. I must survive, people are counting on me and I can not let God down. My clients need me. I do things I don't want to do and I tell myself, 'it's not about me.'"
*~ **Rita** ~*

*"I have to be all in because I have a fear of failure. Even as I have gone through circumstances, my business has been all about timing and listening to God. I have a need to succeed." ~ **Rodney** ~*

~Reflections~

Step #7

Understand the Rules of Engagement

"When God leads you to the edge of the cliff, trust Him fully and let go. Only one of two things will happen: Either He will catch you when you fall or He will teach you how to fly!"

~ Unknown Author~

Get Organized

Know Your Rhythm

Define What Success Means to You

For-Profit versus Nonprofit

Multi-level Marketing versus Entrepreneurship

Let's Talk Legal

Basic Steps in Starting Your Business

Certifications

Get Organized

When I began to develop my current business, it was like walking into a library and starving for knowledge. Where in the world does one begin? I got busy researching and gathering as many resources and tools as I could find from the library, internet, networking groups, community organizations, business-focused programs, webinars, teleconferences, seminars, workshops, symposiums, etc. I was like a kid that heard the ice cream truck coming down the street. I just couldn't get enough.

As I continued to move forward, I recognized I had acquired a great deal of knowledge about my new venture but it would have been so much easier if there was one place I could go to understand where I was and how to get to where I wanted to go. This became my driving force for writing this book for you and other people like us. In the next six chapters, you will find the nuts and bolts of starting and growing your business. Hence, experienced business owners may find some of the information simplistic but my goal is to ensure that this book is user friendly so clarity is essential.

There is so much to grasp but building a business and even more important, building a legacy, takes time. There a three very important points to understand before moving forward: 1. you won't learn everything over night; 2. it will take an extreme amount of focus; 3. it is critical to define what success means to you.

As you continue on this journey, you will experience information overload, especially, if you are in the beginning stages.

There is so much to learn and a plethora of information available especially on the internet. Now is a good time to practice what I refer to as compartmentalization. Create file folders virtually and physically. When you come across information on the internet, file the information in the appropriate folders. When you attend workshops and seminars, gather the information and file it as soon as possible. What you will find is that you may not be able to digest the information or use it during this particular phase in your business but there will come a time when the information will be needed.

In order to focus and stay on course, you will want to grab a notebook or two preferably with tabs and dividers. This is where you will capture and organize your thoughts. This is also a good tool to use when you attend training sessions. You must know, I am considered "old school" and I work best with pen and paper. However, I do realize we are in the age of technology. So, your tablet or laptop may work better for you. Although technology has many advantages, I found that even when my technology is down, I can keep on working.

Know Your Rhythm

Another area that will assist with your focus is to learn your rhythm. In a 24 hour period, everyone has their peak hours of performance, a timeframe in which they operate at maximum efficiency. You must know your body's requirement for rest. If you are an early riser, then I want to introduce you to the 5 O'clock Club, taught by the late, Mary Kay Ash, founder of Mary Kay Cosmetics, Inc. It is amazing the amount of work you can produce by getting your day started at 5:00 a.m. versus 6 or 7 a.m. This is a time when everyone is still asleep and you can maneuver uninterrupted. If done consistently, it feels like you can almost create an 8th day of the week. But the key is to get plenty of rest so that means retiring at a decent hour.

You may be the type of person who thrives on working in the midnight hours. If so, keep in mind, you want to be alert and at your best when dealing with clients; therefore, you will want to adjust your schedule to rest accordingly.

Hopefully, you have decided to add a coach or business consultant to your Success Team. He or she will be able to help you achieve your goals more expeditiously. A knowledgeable professional can help you stay focused, develop your plan, keep you on track and provide you with the necessary resources. If you choose a different route, do yourself a favor and at least identify a mentor or someone in your industry who can assist you. Entrepreneurship can be a lonely road but having someone to help you stay focused and work within your rhythm will prove to be invaluable.

Define What Success Means to You

Now that you have some organization in place and some basics to help you with focus, it's critical to define what success means to you. Is it when you generate $10,000 a month consistently? Does it mean taking your family on frequent vacations? Perhaps, it means having a high customer retention rate because they are satisfied with your products or services.

Only you know when you will feel successful and accomplished. But, it's important to define it, write it down and review it often. It will help drive your mission and vision and guide the foundation of your business. It's also important to clarify because it's very easy to compare yourself to others and knowing what your success factors are will keep you driving in your own lane.

For-Profit versus Nonprofit

The first question to ask yourself is, "Do you plan to make money to give to yourself, your employees, company and/or your shareholders?" If you answered, yes, then you want to start a for-profit business. There are different categories of for-profit businesses. Do you want to purchase a franchise, buy a business that has already been established or create your own? There are pros and cons to all three. Minimally, a franchise can be very costly; however, they typically have excellent training and support available. It also has a proven track record for success which means they have an effective plan of action and name recognition.

If you are considering purchasing someone else's business, it has already been established which may work in your favor and you may be able to purchase it at a reasonable cost. However, the critical question to consider is why the owner wants to sell. It may already have an established customer base and name recognition or you may be inheriting a business that will require damage control and repair because of a tarnished brand.

As an organic entrepreneur, you will be starting your business with your own skill sets, resources, and know-how. The sacrifice in time, money, energy, and resources will be huge but the rewards will be great.

A nonprofit business has great rewards as well but there are distinct differences. The biggest differentiator is the distribution and management of profits. A for-profit generates revenue to make money and a non-profit generates money for a specific cause or community-based initiative. In addition, non-profits are much more closely regulated by the government and funding sources.

The most common non-profit is a 501(c) (3) organization. It is an Internal Revenue Service (IRS) classification of being either a private foundation or public charity. Any distribution of profits must be designated to further the mission of the organization. A great benefit of having a 501(c) (3) organization is receiving charitable contributions which are tax-deductible and the organization is exempt from business income and property taxes.

Multi-Level Marketing versus Entrepreneurship

Being an independent business owner has a long list of benefits and so does starting a business with a multi-level marketing company (MLM). As an independent consultant with Mary Kay Cosmetics, Inc. for almost 20 years, I gained some of the best experience and training I've ever had. As a matter of fact, it has made me who I am today and the truth be told, I landed my previous jobs because of the skill sets I learned in Mary Kay Cosmetics.

Typically, it's less costly to join an MLM and they already have systems in place to help you succeed. They provide training, support, and offer multiple streams of income. Mary Kay Cosmetics, Inc. has one of the best compensation plans available and many MLM companies adopt their model. In Mary Kay, you receive compensation from selling the product, sharing the opportunity to join the company and moving into leadership. You also receive tons of other perks like prizes and recognition.

When considering an MLM, you want to keep several things in mind. First of all, decide what works best for you. Would you like to make a residual income but don't necessarily have the time, energy or resources to start and run a company on your own? Do you tend to be more conservative, like to play it safe or need a more structured environment with proven success? If you answered yes to the two previous questions, a MLM might be best for you.

The next consideration is the length of time a company has been in business. There are MLM companies cropping up every day and they are here today and gone tomorrow, so be cautious. Another huge consideration is the amount of the investment and the compensation plan. How much is the investment, what is the expected return on investment and how often do you need to reinvest? What are the company's expectations? There are many other considerations but the most important one is the compensation plan. Is the focus solely recruitment or do they also sell a beneficial product or service? If its sole focus is recruitment then it is not a solid MLM and can be considered a pyramid; hence, it is a great possibility that company will face legal issues and not be in business for very long.

As an independent business owner, you have yourself, your Success Team, your creative genius, intelligence, and the sweat of your brow to pursue your passion. There is no cookie-cutter approach and people who choose this route typically are risk-takers. It is truly a grassroots operation but when you are operating in your purpose and making a difference in the lives of others, it is well worth the effort.

Let's Talk Legal

Deciding how to structure your business can be a daunting task. This information serves to provide you with the basic knowledge and you are encouraged to consult your attorney or other qualified professional. Please know the requirements differ from state to state or if you live outside of the United States. Therefore, it is best to learn what your county, city, and state or province require before making a decision. Special permits and licensure may also be required and can vary depending on your industry such as privilege license, signs and zoning.

If you reside in the United States, the federal government requires most businesses to have an FEIN (Federal Employee Identification Number). Businesses are responsible for federal and state income taxes. You may also have to consider payroll, sales and use taxes and retail and wholesale sales taxes. Later in this section, you will be given specific information on how to obtain a FEIN.

Other considerations include incorporating your business, establishing an Assumed Name for your business, acquiring insurance and protecting intellectual property.

Before deciding on your business structure, decide if you will share your business with a partner or partners. If so, make sure there is a partnership agreement written and signed by both parties. An attorney can assist you. You will want to make sure the document gives a comprehensive listing of expectations of both parties and includes the exit strategy among many other considerations.

Other considerations regarding partnerships are: Reliability, trustworthiness; work ethic; resourcefulness; attitude and productive behaviors. Do they compliment your strengths and weakness and vice versa? Although seasons in people's lives change, does their life allow them to take on additional responsibility? Does their vision, mission and goals align with yours? There are many other areas to consider based on your needs and the company's needs and goals.

There are three main types of business structures: Sole Proprietorship (the unincorporated business is owned and operated by one person); Partnership: General or Limited (two or more people share in the ownership and operations of the business); or Corporation. Corporations are divided into three categories: Subchapter S Corporation, Subchapter C Corporation, and Limited Liability companies. A Limited Liability Company is a combination of Corporation and Partnership. Each has pros and cons. Please consult with your attorney and/or tax advisor to determine which is best for you.

Steps to Starting Your Business

- If you are outside of Charlotte, North Carolina, check your local county, city, state, or province requirements

1. **Create /prepare several names to search**

   Ideally, the name of your business should represent the type of business you have; it should be easy to remember and offer flexibility for branding purposes.

2. **Conduct an Assumed Name Search and Register Name**

   The purpose of the search is to ensure there is not another business in existence with your business name. Typically, the search is free.

   Register of Deeds
   720 E. 4th St.
   (704) 336-2443
   M-F 8:30 a.m. – 4:30 p.m.
   Cost of Assumed Name: $25

3. **Decide business structure**
   Sole Proprietor
   LLC Partnerships
   Limited Partnerships
   Business Corporations
   Non-profit

4. **Apply for Articles of Organization**
   www.secretary.state.nc.us/corporations/
   NC Department of the Secretary of State
   (919) 807-2225/ (919) 807-2000

Do name search

Print documents from website

Cost: $125 (Documents should be completed and mailed with the fee unless other options are available)

5. **Apply for an Federal Employee Identification Number (FEIN)** www.irs.gov (Free)

Go under "Online Services"

Go to Apply for an Employer Identification Number (EIN)

6. **Apply for Business Privilege License**

Business Tax Office: M – F 9:00 a.m. – 5:00 p.m.

700 N. Tryon St.

(704) 432-4200

.60 per $1,000

(Based on gross revenue – renewable yearly)

7. **Home Occupation Permit**

(If establishing business in a home office)

Business Tax Office

700 N. Tryon St.

(704) 432-4390

Cost: $125 (One time fee)

8. **Obtain Sales and Use Tax ID** (If products will be sold)

Form #NC – BR

(704) 519 – 3000

*Pay business tax bi-annually

*Annual Report due April 15 of each year - $200

Certifications

The majority of the certifications below are for the state of North Carolina. Please check your local area for certifications. Once you become certified with a particular entity, you are able to bid on contractual opportunities. Minority qualifications are also listed below.

Once certified, be sure to check with each entity to see if they require additional vendor information or have an application process to be placed on their vendor list. For example, once certified with Mecklenburg County, you must also submit a vendor application to the finance department so they will know how to process your payment. Also, be sure to research if special licensure/certifications are required for your product or service. If you are an independent contractor or freelancer, it will require Form W-9 which can be found at: www.irs.gov/pub/irs-pdf/fw9.pdf.

Small Business Enterprise Certification
www.charlottebusinessresources.com
The Charlotte Business Resources
Obtaining SBE Certification allows the opportunity for small businesses with the Charlotte Regional Area to grow and be competitive when competing for city contracts.

The Charlotte Business INClusion program
www.charlottebusinessresources.com
The Charlotte Business INClusion program is designed to promote diversity, inclusion, and local business opportunities in the City's contracting and procurement process for businesses headquartered in the Charlotte area.

State of North Carolina Department of Administration
www.doa.state.nc.us/hub

NC Statewide Uniform Certification
A centralized certification process for minority, women and disabled business enterprises managed by the Office of Historically Underutilized Businesses (HUB). Firms are certified as HUB/MWBE (Minority and Woman Business Enterprise) and their information is compiled in a Statewide Uniform Certification (SWUC) Vendor database.

North Carolina Department of Transportation Certifications
www.connect.ncdot.gov/business

NCDOT Small Business Enterprise (SBE) Certification
Certain NCDOT projects under $500,000 are made available for exclusive bidding by certified SBE firms, thereby eliminating competition from large firms. Business revenue must be less than $1.5 million.

NCDOT Disadvantaged Business Enterprise (DBE) Certification
The U.S. Department of Transportation (USDOT) has had in effect for more than 20 years a policy of helping small businesses owned and controlled by socially and economically disadvantaged individuals, including minorities and women, in participating in contracting opportunities created by DOT financial assistance programs. To help administer this policy, the NCDOT verifies that businesses meet the requirements of the program by certifying businesses as DBE firms.

NCDOT prequalification considerations:

DBE – Disadvantaged Business Enterprise
A Disadvantaged Business Enterprise is a small, independent business that is at least 51% owned by one or more socially or economically disadvantaged individuals. At least one of these owners must control

the firm's management and daily operations, and the owners must share in the risks and profits commensurate with their ownership interest.

SBE - Small Business Enterprise
The Small Business Enterprise Program, hereinafter referred to as SBE Program, was developed to provide contract opportunities for firms that meet the eligibility criteria, to compete against others that are comparably positioned in their industries and markets. This program gives smaller businesses with annual gross incomes up to $1.5 million, excluding materials, the opportunity to participate in NCDOT construction projects.

MBE/WBE Program
Minority Business Enterprise/Women Business Enterprise
Through the Minority Business Enterprise/Women Business Enterprise Program, the North Carolina Department of Transportation ensures firms that meet the eligibility requirements are afforded the maximum opportunity to participate in the performance of contracts financed with state funds.

SPSF - Small Professional Services Firm
The SPSF Program was developed to provide sub-consulting opportunities for firms that meet the eligibility criteria. Small businesses determined to be eligible for participation in the SPSF program are those meeting size standards defined by Small Business Administration (SBA) regulations.

The SPSF program is a race, ethnicity, and gender neutral program designed to increase the availability of contracting opportunities for small businesses on federal and state funded contracts.

HUB – Historically Underutilized Businesses
The HUB Office certifies minorities, women, persons with disabilities, socially and economically disadvantaged individuals, and disabled

business enterprises as historically underutilized business firms for North Carolina State Government via online vendor registration.

Historically Underutilized Businesses (HUBs) as defined in N.C. General Statutes 143-48.4, and 143-128.4 (a), and (b) are minority, women, disabled and disadvantaged owned businesses that are at least 51 percent owned and controlled by one of the aforementioned groups. The HUB Office also promotes the utilization of disabled business enterprises and non-profit work centers for the blind and severely disabled by state agencies and public entities.

Carolinas-Virginia Minority Supplier Development Council
www.cvmsdc.org
(CVMSDC) promotes and facilitates business relationships between the public/private sector and certified minority-owned businesses.

Women Business Enterprise National Council
www.wbenc.org
Becoming certified as a WBENC will allow help to promote your company to major corporations actively seeking to contract with a woman/woman owned business.

US Small Business Administration
www.sba.gov
Under the **8 (a) Business Development Program,** the SBA certifies small businesses considered to be socially and economically disadvantaged under its nine year 8(a) Business Development Program. The program provides government contracting opportunities, as well as, one-to-one counseling, training, workshops and management and technical guidance.

~Reflections~

Step #8

Build a Solid Foundation

"And the Lord answered me, and said, 'Write the vision, and make it plain upon tables, that he may run that readeth it.' "

~ Habakkuk 2:2 ~

Asking the Right Questions

Develop Company Foundation

Develop Your Product or Service

Identify Target Market

Competitive Research Analysis

Conduct Feasibility Study

Develop a Marketing Plan

Develop a Business Plan

Asking the Right Questions

After you have determined your product or service is marketable and has potential to make a profit, determined your business structure, finalized your Articles of Incorporation, and secured your FEIN (if applicable), now it's time to establish a relationship with a bank and set up a bank account for your new business. At minimum, you will need your identification, Articles of Incorporation, FEIN (if applicable) and funds to establish the account.

Identify several financial institutions in order to compare the product lines, especially their fees and accessibility of funds, and requirements for business loans (if applicable). Be sure to determine the needs of your business before selecting a financial institution. Read the fine print and understand the banks' policies including closing accounts. You want to avoid banks that charge fees to close accounts or excessive fees in other areas. If you have not already created or considered your personal budget, now is a good time to do so. In this step, you will also focus on creating a budget which will be included in your business plan.

If you have not already connected with SCORE (Service Corps of Retired Executives), now is a good time to visit a SCORE office and find out about their workshops, consultations and other resources for small businesses. SCORE is a resource partner with the U.S. Small Business Administration. It is a non-profit association that gives free mentoring to small businesses. I found them extremely beneficial.

In fact, I was assigned to a counselor who has become the best mentor I could ever have hoped for. He gave me a helpful guide I used as a checklist during my planning phases: Business Start-Up Resource Guide: Starting a Business in North Carolina published by the University of North Carolina's Small Business and Technology Development Center (SBTDC). You can download a free copy at: www.sbtdc.org/pdf/startup.pdf.

Begin interviewing attorneys and accountants. Depending on the type of business you have, you may require several different types of attorneys. Legal advice can be very costly so a cost effective solution is Legal Shield. I have utilized their services since the beginning and have sought the help of different types of attorneys for a nominal monthly fee.

When interviewing accountants, consider fees along with the questions by Jane Porter on January 14, 2013 and posted on m.entrepreneur.com, 10 Questions to Ask Before Hiring a Tax Accountant

1. What kinds of clients do you work with?
2. Are you available year round?
3. What's your experience with the IRS?
4. Who will be doing the work?
5. Are you a conservative or more aggressive accountant?
6. How do you bill for your services?
7. How do you handle working with multiple entities?
8. Can you tell me about medical expense reimbursement plan?

9. What tax program do you use?

10. How often will we communicate about tax issues?

You may also want to inquire about credentials, bookkeeping services, experience in working with small businesses, and the response time when servicing your company. Ask about the computerized accounting system recommended for your type of business. Recommendations from existing clients and a commitment to continuing education can also help guide your selection.

In addition, consider the advice they offer beyond basic cost-cutting strategies and if they outsource to other companies or individuals. Do they do tax audits and small business loan applications? Most importantly, how familiar are they with current tax laws and accounting practices? Ask them to provide you with a full list of fees, charges, and additional fees you have not considered. If you plan to do your own bookkeeping, Quickbooks seems to be the most popular software because its easy to use and cost-effective. However, you might consider a basic excel spreadsheet if you are just starting out. Minimally, you need to track your income and expenses. Consult with your accountant or bookkeeper regarding how to set up your bookkeeping according to your type of business.

Remember, your attorney and accountant are critical to your Success Team as are your business coach/consultant, marketing and branding expert, web designer, as well as, other experts. Be thorough in your research and be prepared with the right questions so you can get the desired results. After all, the success of your business depends on you and you depend on your Success Team to provide you with the most effective and efficient resources to support you and help achieve your goals.

Develop Company Foundation

Building the foundation of your company is one of the most critical steps in developing a successful business. It also ensures you remain true to each element in the foundation. In order to create a strong foundation, you will want to define your ultimate vision or BHAG, purpose/mission, core values, brand promise, and your targets.

In 1994, James Collins and Jerry Porras wrote Built to Last: Successful Habits of Visionary Companies and coined the term BHAG. Big Hairy Audacious Goal or BHAG is a strategic business statement which defines a company or project's mid to long term goal. It may sound like an outlandish idea to those outside of the organization or project but the parties responsible for making it happen, believe the goal is achievable. Do you seek to build a strong international presence in your business or to become a multi-million dollar company in the next five years? It is possible if you put the appropriate foundation in place and utilize the right resources at the right time and with the right people.

Exactly why are you in business? What is your driving force for being in business? Once you have clarity on these two questions, you will have identified your Purpose (mission) or core of the business. Everyone in your company should know, embrace, and exhibit your purpose. All decisions made should have your purpose (mission) at the center.

Corporate America labels this next very important concept, "corporate culture." Your Core Values determine how you and/or your employees carry out the work of the business. It is usually comprised of 5 -7 statements which reflect your company's values and can be used as one of the tools to guide which decisions should or should not be made.

When you think about your ideal customer or client, what need does your company satisfy better than the competition and how do you differentiate yourself from the competition? The answer becomes your "brand promise." It is your commitment to honoring and constantly refining what drives your business.

Now, let's talk Targets. Where do you want your business to be one, three, five and thirty years from today? Revisit your BHAG and consider profitability, revenue, employees, new products or lines of service, expansions and possible collaborations.

Developing Your Product or Service

The success of your business depends on the viability of your products and/or services. Is there a need for your products or services? Essentially, what will the consumer think about it and what do they really want or need? Will your product or service create a buzz? How likely is the consumer to tell their family and friends or in today's technology put it on Twitter, Pinterest or their Facebook page?

There are so many new products and services launching in the marketplace every day that it becomes increasingly challenging to attract clients. You want your business to be a magnet so people will want to pay for what you have to offer. You may have the best product in the world but until it attracts people and provides a solution for a need or pain that's ailing them, your product or service is just another idea. Think like a doctor or researcher and how your product or service provides a cure. Paint a picture of the problem to solve and decide how it will look when you solve it.

Make sure you are completely transparent with your product or service and make it easy for your customers or clients to know how their money is being spent and how the product or service will benefit them. Product pricing and packaging is key and you want to do your due diligence so that your product or service is attractive and affordable but competitively priced. Determining the price on your product or service can be challenging but your competitive research analysis should prove to be very beneficial.

Before conducting a feasibility study, brainstorm about the many different ways your products can be used and services provided. Once you have completed a feasibility study of each, you will have created multiple streams of income if there seems to be a need for them. In addition, keep an open mind about possible collaborations with other businesses that will enhance and/or leverage what you have to offer. If you decide to barter (exchange each other's services or goods without the exchange of money), establish guidelines and follow them.

Determine Target Market

A target market is a specific population on which a company focuses its marketing strategies in order to promote and sell a product or service. Determining your target market requires an identification of potential clients or customers within a specified industry and a competitive research analysis. The U.S. Census Bureau is a great resource.

In determining your target market, you need to examine potential clients' or customers' *psychographics,* the study of personality, opinions, attitudes, values, interests, and lifestyles and *demographics,* which is quantifiable statistics such as age, income, marital status, ethnicity, etc.

Minimally, here are a few questions for your consideration: What are the ages, household income, ethnicity and marital status of potential clients? Do they have children, if so, how many and how old are they? How do they think? What influences their buying decisions? Where do they live, shop, eat, work, exercise, etc? What types of hobbies do they have? What need does my product or service satisfy?

Ultimately, your product or service must help your potential clients or customers save money, time, or energy; heal; grow; fulfill a desire or need or be more effective and efficient. Create a profile of your ideal customers and clients so you clearly understand how to position your product or service as you begin to market.

Competitive Research Analysis

The next phase is to actually conduct a competitive research analysis. Begin with these key questions of at least your top five competitors and be specific in your responses. The most efficient resource is their company website. You will also want to gather any marketing collateral (brochures, pamphlets, flyers, etc.) available.

1. What product or services do they offer and how long have they been in business?
2. What makes them unique?
3. What is their brand and is it easy to identify?
4. Who do they serve?
5. What makes your products or services different?

Conduct a Feasibility Study

A feasibility study examines the viability of a product or service. If done in the beginning, a comprehensive feasibility study can save time, money and resources in determining profitability of a product or service. It may also reveal different ideas not previously considered.

Be careful with whom you share your product or service idea unless you can trust them and they are supportive. On the other hand, as you share your idea, your cheerleaders may think it's a great idea but when you test the market, it may not be as popular. So, here are a few areas to consider when starting your feasibility study:

1. The ultimate goal is to determine if there is a demand for your product or service.

2. Research other companies providing the same product or services in your area.

3. Research the resources needed to make the product or provide the services and to complete a comprehensive study.

4. Determine the cost of producing the product or service.

5. Project the profit and financial feasibility.

The study will also require a market analysis. According to dictionary.com, a market analysis is the process of determining factors, conditions, and characteristics of a market. You may also utilize questionnaires and surveys depending on what works best to achieve the goal.

Consider doing a marketing analysis annually and include potential clients not just existing clients served. A great resource to consider using can be found at: www.http://m.wikihow.com/write-a-market-analysis.

In order to develop a company that has longevity and is competitive in the market place, a SWOT Analysis should be included in your feasibility study. A SWOT Analysis is a thorough assessment of Strengths, Weaknesses, Opportunities, and Threats for you and your product or service which will help create a sustainable competitive advantage. On the next couple of pages are a few questions to get you started.

SWOT Analysis

Strengths

What is your strongest business asset?

What do you do well?

What unique resources can you draw upon?

What do others see as your strengths?

What makes your product or service viable?

What makes your product or service stand out?

What makes your product or service unique?

Weaknesses

What could you improve?

Where do you have fewer resources than others?

What are others likely to see as weaknesses?

What can be improved?

In what areas does the competition have an edge?

What does business need to make it more effective?

Opportunities

What opportunities are available or can you create?

How can you turn your strengths into opportunities?

What trends do you see in your industry?

What trends do you foresee?

What trends could you take advantage of?

How might those trends impact your business?

How can you leverage it?

Threats

What is the competition doing?

What are the obstacles?

How can you leverage the obstacles?

What threats could harm you?

What threats do your weaknesses expose you to?

There are many other areas to consider as you conduct your feasibility study and a qualified professional can assist you. However, if you decide to take on this project, there are many examples of feasibility studies. One I found helpful comes from The Food and Agriculture Organization of the United Nations. It can be viewed in their Corporate Document Repository entitled Guidelines for Small-scale Fruit and Vegetable Processors. The website is http:/www. fao.org/3/aw6864e/w6864e09.htm#2.3.conductinga feasibility study.

Develop a Marketing Plan

Marketing is conducting a variety of activities created to reach and fulfill a need of a specific target audience for the purpose of selling a product, service or promoting an event. It is imperative to understand an effective marketing plan requires a variety of activities done on a consistent basis until the goal is reached. Most importantly, it must be designed with the client or customer in mind.

Now it's time to put the research to the test by developing a well-developed marketing plan. You will utilize the information gathered in developing your product and service and the research on your target market, competitors, and in your feasibility study to create a comprehensive marketing strategy. The strategy or plan will also include your products, services, branding, promotions, networking or prospecting, publicity, public relations, cross promotion/marketing, advertising, distribution, pricing, sales, and customers.

Consider the important elements below as you strategize on the most important aspect of your business: Marketing. If you have completed the previous questions, you already have much of the required information.

Begin by defining the share of the market you expect to capture along with a sales revenue forecast. Then list the specific products or services offered along with the prices and features for each. A range of price points is advisable because it gives you the potential to up-sell (customer buys more than just one product or service).

Based on your client profile, list at least 5 or 6 places your target audience frequents and how you can connect with them. For instance, if they work out at the local exercise facility, perhaps you can talk to the management of that establishment about doing drawings for free or discounted products or services. If it is a business, determine its size based on the annual sales, number of staff, and the number of locations. Do your best to identify the decision maker and how best to connect with him or her.

Create a list of the top five or ten reasons why your target market will buy your product or service and the advantages you have over the competition. Utilize information from your surveys or questionnaires if they have been completed.

The most challenging task is getting the right message to the right audience. Determine how your target market will find out about your product or service. Create your messaging for turning them from prospective customers into satisfied clients who will be repeat customers. How you will follow up?

Make sure your plan is written out and includes your mission, objective, budget and responsibilities. It should be no longer than one page long and be very specific with the marketing activity schedule, targeted dates, resources needed, follow up strategy and to whom it has been assigned.

When creating your plan, consider offline, as well as, online marketing strategies. Offline strategies include: Advertising, networking events, phone calls, magazines, newspapers, television, radio and presentations, etc. Online strategies include advertising, newsletters, LinkedIn, Facebook, Twitter, Pinterest, etc.

Consider the distribution of your product or service, as well as, new orders, returns and inquiries from clients. Determine your credit policies, required payment schedule, if you will allow the customer to pay at a later date and how you will handle slow paying clients or customers. Product storage, handling and shipping and materials for packaging must also be taken into account as well. Include the cost and fees for accepting credit card payments. Paypal and Square Up are two cost effective services.

A public relations plan should also be included in your marketing plan. Public relations or PR is often overlooked in small business because it is misunderstood. If done correctly, PR is designed to reach your target audience in order to gain exposure and build rapport with your customers, potential customers and the community. An effective plan leverages topics of public interest and news items to increase your company's visibility and help your target audience feel connected to your brand. On the other hand, it can also be used to counter negative publicity. In this case, a public relations expert is recommended.

Develop a Business Plan

Business Plans are roadmaps to chart your company's success. Essentially, it includes forecasts for three to five years, a business and marketing model, and profit and growth plan. It is referred to as a "living document" because it is ever changing. It is not only used to determine the direction of a company, define necessary activities or tasks but it can also be used to secure working capital, loans or investors for your business. Three of the most important people from your Success Team to help create a solid business plan are a business strategist and marketing and finance or accounting experts. A wealth of comprehensive business plan templates can be found at:

www.bplans.com. You can identify a company that offers products or services similar to yours and use it as a model. The key is to keep it as simple but as thorough as possible. If you are planning to open a brick and mortar business, it is imperative to complete a more comprehensive business plan to ensure consideration has been given to every area. However, if you are not and need economical office space, consider incubators or Executive Office Suites locations. These facilities tend to have office and meeting space and additional areas conducive for conducting workshops or other larger scale events.

Earlier, I shared the Business Start-Up Resource Guide produced by the Small Business and Technology Development Center. I found it extremely helpful for writing my business plan as well. This process can be very time consuming but the great news is you already have several critical components completed which should put you a step ahead.

~Reflections~

Powerhouse in Motion

Step #9:

Make Your Brand Come to Life

"Don't sit down and wait for the opportunities to come.

Get up and make them!" ~ Madam CJ Walker ~

What's Branding?

Name and Logo Development

Website Development

Business Cards

Email and Phone Communication

Press Kits and Image

Social Media Strategy

What's Branding?

Marketing is the lifeline of your business but branding is the lifeline of your marketing plan. The American Marketing Association (AMA) defines a brand as a name, term, sign, symbol or design, or a combination of them intended to identify the goods and services of one seller or group of sellers and to differentiate from those of other sellers.

In Laura Lakes' article entitled: What is Branding and How Important is it to Your Marketing Strategy, she outlined the objectives of a good brand:

1. Delivers the message clearly
2. Confirms your credibility
3. Connects your target prospects emotionally
4. Motivates the buyer
5. Concretes User Loyalty

In addition, your brand should deliver consistent messaging across all marketing collateral, publicity, public relations campaigns, internal and external communications, marketing, and advertising efforts. This includes your website, letterhead, logos, business cards, social media platforms and press kits, etc.

Chief Branding Strategist Re Perez said that emotions lead to action and reasons lead to conclusions. You will have 20% naysayers who won't do business with you, 60% will follow you and 20% will love you. Therefore, your brand strategies should target the 80% and leverage emotion. Emotions drive people to make a decision to buy.

Authenticity is another extremely important element in branding. People need to be able to connect or feel you and your company's brand. It should evoke positive thoughts and responses. If you are interested in defining your authentic brand, a great resource is the book Branding the Authentic You: Building a Conscious-Centered Brand & Lifestyle That Speaks To Your Extraordinary Self by Elyshia Brooks.

Name and Logo Development

By now, you should already have your name and the research should have been done with the County and State. You should also do a Google search to make sure it is not a trademarked name or too close to another name in your search. If so, you want to alter it for distinction so your target market will not be directed to the other company's site. You want to also take a close look at their logo to make sure your company logo is different and can not be easily confused with the competition.

Your name and logo should be unique to you and represent your company's brand and image. Ideally, it should be short and catchy so it's easily remembered and reflects the type of products and services your company offers. The colors chosen should be complimentary to the name, company brand, and appeal to your target audience. This helps to market more effectively.

When designing your company logo, create the same logo several different ways and in different lighter and darker color schemes and variations. Solicit the opinion of others. Because your logo will be used on all materials, be sure to test how it looks very small and very large. It should be crisp, clean and appealing.

Website Development

Website development can be compared to a brick and mortar building but it's online. Instead of your customer or client coming to you, it is your opportunity to go directly to them anywhere, 24 hours a day. If done correctly, it can be a powerful lead generating tool and drive company profits.

Your website developer is another important person on your Success Team. Finding the right web designer for your team is critical. Take a look at several, review their websites and interview them. Take notes as you research their websites and compare the following: Website's professional and user friendly quality, appeal, creativity, variety, pricing, timeframe for project completion, and if they write content or provide a resource. It is also important to ask if they offer maintenance service and if so, what type. Request their prices.

Next, make an appointment to speak with each web designer. Find out if they do everything in house or if they outsource. You may also inquire about their client recommendations and if they provide social media services such as blogging. Be sure to ask if they will integrate your website with your social media platforms like Twitter, Facebook and LinkedIn. As a result, when you blog, it will appear simultaneously on all connected mediums. If not, you can also integrate them yourself by using Hoot Suite or Twitter Feed.

Establishing your website will require securing a domain name and hosting for your website. Your website developer may offer that service. If not, there are many to choose from and some are free but I found www.domainforsuccess.com to be cost effective and their staff is always available. You must do a name search to make sure that particular domain name is not already in use. You will be able to create multiple email addresses once it's established.

Business Cards

Presenting your business card says the doors are now open for business. In the developmental stages, identify a company that is creative, easy to work with and competitively priced. Once you convey your ideas, the design of the business card should reflect your company brand. The same company should also be able to create company letterhead. Vistaprint.com has many product lines available and is an economical option.

If you don't have a brick and mortar business and you work from home, consider setting up a mailbox at a UPS Store. The difference between the post office mailboxes and the UPS Store vary greatly. The post office mailboxes are less expensive and your address will indicate a P.O. Box. At times, this can present an issue because sometimes you won't be able to get deliveries at a P.O. Box.

An effective alternative is setting up a mailbox at a UPS Store which is more costly but it gives you an actual address which can be more appealing. You can access them 24/7 and there is always someone there to sign or accept larger packages during office hours. Either way, you will want your address listed on your business cards along with your name, title, contact numbers, email, social media platforms, company name, logo and website.

Email and Phone Communication

When you start your business, you may want to establish a professional email instead of one generated on Google or other platforms. Your email address represents your brand. In order to create a signature email address you want to establish a domain name and hosting which will give you multiple emails and a platform for your website.

An email signature appears at the end of your email messages and should also be a marketing platform. An effective email signature includes your name, title, company name, logo if possible, your contact numbers, and how they can connect with you on social media. A quote always adds a nice touch and helps people relate to you.

Email is an effective marketing tool but it can also be damaging to your brand if not used correctly. Always be brief when creating messages and most importantly, check spelling and grammar. No matter how frequently you correspond in a day's time, it is always refreshing to be addressed by name versus just beginning with the content of the message. Reserve difficult conversations for face to face or phone communication. Email is not the appropriate medium because thoughts and ideas may be misconstrued.

When forwarding emails, remove the other names present in the address and content fields and blind copy if it's a group of people unless it's appropriate to keep the names visible.

As you are networking, there may come a time that you want to connect one individual to another. First of all, consider asking the person to whom you are connecting the individual for their permission and let them know prior to the introduction. When sending the email, be concise in stating the purpose of the connection and some positive aspects about each individual to create a warmer connection.

Another important branding opportunity is phone communication. When answering your business line, you will want to greet the person on the other line so well that they can feel your smile and warmth through the telephone line. Professionalism is a must the moment you pick up the phone because this can make or break a relationship with a client or prospective client. Create a concise greeting. For example, "Great morning, thank you for calling (name of company), this is (your name). How may I help you?"

Your outgoing voicemail greeting is an excellent way to invite new customers and make current customers feel good about their relationship with your company. Your messages should be professional, concise, and welcoming. Most importantly, they should reflect your brand. It is appropriate to return calls and reply to emails within 24 – 48 hours. When calling others, always be professional in tone and speech. After the initial greeting, ask if the other person has a moment before speaking and always be prepared and have a plan for the call in terms of your expected outcome.

Press Kits and Image

Press kits are a great way to tell your company's story and help your target audience learn about the person behind the company. It is an essential piece to your branding and marketing. If you ever desire to speak or gain media exposure, you will want to have a well-written and concise press kit. Minimally, your press kits should contain: A press release about your product or service, your bio and summary of your company's products or services, possible media questions and talking points if applicable.

One great lesson I learned from Glenn Proctor, an editor for over 40 years and a member of a Pulitzer Prize winning team, is to build relationships with the media. You begin this process by retrieving or creating a list of media from radio, television and newspapers. Connect with the editor or a decision maker with radio and TV over coffee or lunch. Allow them to get to know you. When you send your press release, you won't be a stranger.

Always represent your company well in your thinking, dress, speaking, and the way you interact with people. You are your brand and your brand means everything to your company. When in public always wear what you sell. So, if you own a cosmetic company, your face becomes advertising. If you have a sports apparel store, you should be a walking billboard. If you own a hair salon or barber shop, your hair should look healthy and serve as an attraction magnet.

Undoubtedly, you may have negative experiences in working with the public. Always remember, you are your company and you always want to represent it in a positive light twenty-four hours a day and seven days a week. Establish your company as a company that delivers superior quality with professionalism and punctuality. If you don't offer a particular product or service, let your customer know. If you commit to a timeframe, stick to it and if you find you can not deliver as originally stated, simply communicate it to your customer and offer a gift or discount on a future purchase. This will go a long way with customer retention and satisfaction.

Social Media Strategy

First of all, if you are new to social media it is a world all by itself and can be overwhelming to say the least. I strongly suggest you take workshops or add a social media expert to your Success Team. An expert can educate you and help develop a strategy to best utilize social media to grow your business. Be patient with yourself because it is a process.

Essentially, social media connects you and your business to the world and if you don't utilize it, you will be missing out on revenue generating opportunities. If embraced, the world becomes your oyster and you will be able to reach your target market more consistently and effectively because social media has become the standard of communication.

However, as you increase your capacity and bandwidth in the world of social media, you will need to set up accounts with passwords and there will be many. Be sure to organize all of the accounts and passwords in a safe and specific area that is easily accessible to you.

There are many types of social media but the most popular are Facebook, LinkedIn and Twitter. Email communication is also an extremely useful tool. Facebook will help you connect with your target market. However, you will want to separate your business from your personal page. You have the opportunity to build your network, share your message, and join other communities to increase your visibility and advertise.

LinkedIn is an excellent venue for networking with other professionals and joining groups in your industry. You can post newsletters and other information. It's a great recruiting tool if you are looking for employees and it allows you to post jobs and manage your search.

Twitter is designed for quick communication to get a specific message to your target audience. It's an effective way to keep your company name in front of your audience and build your brand.

Your website and/or blog are important aspects of your social media strategy. Blogging can be considered as creating relationships with your target audience through the use of sharing information on a consistent basis.

In order to increase your SEO or Search Engine Optimization, which is a strategy used to increase the visibility of a website or a web page, it requires the use of key words and all of the social media platforms working together to drive prospects to the page. Hoot Suite (hootsuite.com) and Twitter Feed (twitterfeed.com) are great tools to connect all platforms. One of the most important lessons I have learned about social media is you must be consistent and these tools help you accomplish that goal.

~Reflections~

Step #10:

Systemize Your Business

Entrepreneurship is living a few years of your life like most people won't, so that you can spend the rest of your life like most people can't." ~ Warren G. Tracy's student ~

Business Operations and Systems

Core Functions

Customer Relations Management

Business Operations can be defined as activities involved in the day to day functions of the business conducted for the purpose of generating profits. As you begin to develop the daily operations of your business, you want to think efficiency, effectiveness, and how to strategically align all functions to support the generation of profit and growth of your company.

As the chief executive officer (CEO), you may also serve as the chief operating officer (COO). The difference between the two is the chief executive officer is the visionary, as such, drives the direction of the company and the chief operations officer leads the operations to ensure the company aligns with the direction of the vision.

If you are just starting out, chances are, you will wear both hats along with many others. However, it's important to spend time on both of these key roles in strategic planning and execution.

Business Systems

A business system is an orderly plan, method or procedure designed to support core business functions. The CEO determines the direction your company is headed, the COO ensures all functions are moving effectively and efficiently to help you arrive at your destination. Business systems give life to the operations and support the essential activities. Below are examples of business systems that generally apply to all businesses. It is not an exhaustive list so you will need to decide the systems your company needs to have in place to operate according to the plan.

Types of Business Systems
> **Marketing**
> **Production**
> **Administrative**
> **Personal/Professional Development**
> Strategic Planning
> Sales/Business Development
> Product Development
> Advertising
> Legal
> Accounting
> Customer Service
> Research
> Training & Development
> Communications
> Technology
> Human Resources

Core Business Functions

One of the toughest challenges of any business owner is managing the multitude of roles every day while making sure the company is producing revenue, building future business and maintaining daily operations.

Core functions are daily and consistent strategic tasks and activities conducted to drive a specific outcome, produce accountability, and ultimately help to generate profit. If utilized, you will build and grow your business.

There are many different types of systems to run a business on a daily basis, but I have found the easiest way to balance all the roles, keep the systems moving forward, and stay focused is utilizing the core business functions concept. There are four core business functions as defined by the Eker Millionaire Mind Intensive T. Harv Eker Signature Program: Marketing, Production, Administrative and Personal. However, I modified it slightly to include professional development because it's imperative business owners stay sharp and prepared.

If you can imagine four quadrants with each of the four core functions divided into each of them. **Marketing** should be placed in the first quadrant and comprise the majority of your daily activity, especially if you are new in business. All marketing in the core functions should be referred to as a concept called, an IPA or Income Producing Activity taught by Mary Kay Ash. This activity requires direct contact or attempts to connect to your target population such as networking, blogging, and following up with potential customers.

The second quadrant is **Production**. Production is any function which creates the product or service your company provides. For example, if you are an accountant, your production would consist of doing taxes or bookkeeping for clients. If you are a speaker, production would be writing speeches or preparing for your presentation. If you design websites, it would mean doing the work to create the website, etc.

The third quadrant is **Administrative**. Administrative function includes activities like preparing invoices, checking email, filing, preparing correspondence, generating reports, or any task considered as office work.

Lastly, the **Personal and Professional Development** quadrant includes time spent spiritually, with family, physical exercise, reading, attending workshops and seminars, etc. Now that the systems and the core functions have been outlined:

1. Identify all systems your company needs
2. Place each system under the appropriate core function
3. Define 3 – 5 important areas in each system
4. Create tools, flowcharts, procedures & policies for each system
5. Assign an owner and timeline

For example, you are the owner of a staffing agency. Below is a model of possible core functions and systems.

Core Functions

Marketing

Attend career fair to recruit temporary and full-time staff and companies needing staff

Production

Identify and call places of employment in which to place your client

Administrative

Flowchart for new client

1. Schedule interview with potential client
2. Create a new client folder
3. Interview client
4. Do background check
5. Find placement for new client

Professional/Personal

Read staffing industry magazine/Run 5 miles on lunch break

Customer Service System

First, identify software or a CRM (Customer Relations Management Tool) to manage and maintain customer base

1. New Client Follow Up Plan

- Send handwritten note after meeting
- Download into Retention System

2. Retention Plan

- Send newsletters monthly
- Call quarterly

These four core business functions along with the assigned systems should guide your daily activities. We will revisit the Core Functions later in Step #12.

Customer Relations Management Tool

A Customer Relations Management (CRM) tool is an essential system or tool used to manage communication with customers, build relationships, increase customer retention and ultimately, generate revenue. It's great to generate customers but it's another challenge to retain them and grow the relationship. A CRM will serve as an extension of you to build your brand and help you reach your target audience consistently.

There are many types of tools and systems available in the market place. Two excellent options are Aweber (www.aweber.com) and Constant Contact (www.constantcontact.com). You will be able to create newsletters, broadcast messages and build your list of potential clients. Both offer tremendous customer service and are readily available.

~ *Reflections* ~

Step #11:

Build Relationships

"I've missed more than 9,000 shots in my career. I've lost almost 300 games, 26 times. I've been trusted to take the game winning shot and missed. I've failed over and over and over again in my life.

And that is why I succeed."

~ Michael Jordan~

The Art of Networking

Building your List

The Science behind the Sale

The Winning Pitch

The Art of Networking

If you talk to many people in business, one of the most common challenges is networking. Networking is meeting new people to build your business but most importantly, build relationships. When you walk into a crowded room full of people who seem to be intimidating, what do you say to break the ice? Who speaks first? How do you get past being nervous? How do you get past feeling like you're selling something? Suffice it to say, I have not come across many people who are totally comfortable with networking, even if they have done it for many years. Each opportunity presents new scenarios and you can never predict the outcome.

The first concept to grasp is you will not build a relationship with everyone and those with whom you connect won't necessarily become a customer but might lead you to someone who will. In addition, everybody who meets your ideal target market criteria, may not need to be a customer because it's too difficult to serve them. Of course, you may not know this until a relationship has been established.

Networking can be fun if you master the basics and are always prepared. Some basics include: Developing a polished and professional elevator speech; being equipped with great business cards and other marketing collateral; and pre-planning the outcome or what you expect to achieve as a result of the networking experience. When you network, you should always have a professional appearance, a nice pen and be prepared to ask the right questions to produce the desired results.

A huge obstacle most new business owners must overcome is being so excited about what you are offering that you talk more than you listen. This is a sure-fire way to make people want to avoid you.

The answers to most of the questions asked at the beginning of this section can be found in building the relationship by asking the right questions to uncover needs of potential clients. Remember consistency is key and it may take 3 to 6 months of scheduled communication before a sale is made. In the meantime, be resourceful so you can refer people to others if you don't have what they need. This is the sign of a true professional.

Lastly, one of the most important elements of successful networking is the follow up. An effective timeframe is within 24 – 48 hours before the person forgets you. If done well, they will be enthused about connecting and hearing more about the product or service you offer to meet their needs.

Building your List

This concept is not new but it has become the new buzz word in social media. It is online networking that builds a list of contacts in order to establish relationships and ultimately, a new client base. This can be achieved in several different ways but driving people to your website and having them opt in is probably one of the most effective and you receive the maximum benefit. Not only does this build your potential customer base but your site's ranking in the social media world is increased which can translate into an increase in business. SEO or search engine optimization can help to make this happen. SEO is maximizing and synchronizing the various social media platforms in order to drive traffic to your website or blog. If you plan to engage in social media, your list will become your most effective marketing tool. You can find great tips at www.experian.com/small-business/how-to-build-an-email-list.jsp but I strongly recommend consulting with a social media expert.

The Science behind the Sale

In the past 30 years, I have sold everything from credit cards and premium meats over the telephone; $5,000 water systems; women's clothing; pharmaceuticals for cardiovascular and alzheimers diseases, epilepsy, depression and diabetes to skin care and color cosmetics. The experiences have been vast and the lessons have been many.

Some of the best practices I found were: Using the right tools at the right time and with the right people, create systems and leverage personality to build the relationships. Selling is all about building relationships so your authenticity must shine through. People don't like to be sold but they do buy from people they know, like and trust. If you want to build customer loyalty and keep clients coming back, find their need and fill it. Offer them a solution to their pain, problem or issue; your authenticity; unbeatable customer service; and quality products at an affordable price and they will return. Not only will they return but they will refer potential clients to you. John C. Maxwell said it best "People don't care how much you know, until they know how much you care." This is the beginning of understanding the psychology or science of selling.

Selling can be scary, especially if you have always said, "I don't like sales." A majority of the people I have encountered have said the same words. However, everyone has the ability to share their enthusiasm and get people on board. When you were a kid, did you ever have a burning desire for something but your parents said "no"? Did your persistence eventually pay off and you got what you wanted? Newsflash: You sold them. They may not have been happy but you still got what you wanted.

In selling, the goal is to have a win-win situation where your product or service is sold to a satisfied client. In order to create a positive experience and outcome for both parties, you must first adjust your mindset from selling to building relationships. Earlier in Step #5, DISC or the Four Temperament Model of Human Behavior was outlined. If you have not already identified your personality type, it will make you much more comfortable in building relationships and allowing your authenticity to shine. Furthermore, it will help you communicate so your potential client will listen, understand, and make a decision to purchase your product or service.

Selling is definitely a balancing act. You must build relation-ships by keeping your pipeline filled with a consistent flow of potential customers but you must also know and work your numbers in order to meet your goal. In order to keep your pipeline filled, relationships must be established with different organizations and you will want to attend networking events on a consistent basis. Asking existing clients for referrals is also effective. These are just a few ways to generate a list of potential clients in the community but don't forget to include your social media opportunities.

When you already know an individual or they were referred to you, they are considered warm leads. If you make calls from the yellow pages or other listing sources, these are referred to as cold leads. When planning your day, it is extremely beneficial to focus on building your warm leads because this is where the return will be greatest.

In order to be an effective salesperson, you must understand the psychology or science of selling and the mechanics of selling like defining your goals, knowing your numbers, securing the relationship in the delivery of the presentation and assuming or closing the sale.

Now that we have covered some basic concepts behind the psychology of the sale, let's take a look at the mechanics of selling. Defining your goal or knowing what you want to have happen with each client is critically important. However, this is driven by your sales goals. Sales goals are decided based on your projections from your business plan which are broken down in annual, quarterly, monthly, and daily goals.

For example: If you've projected $100,000 for the year, you

must produce or sale $8,333 per month, $2,083 per week and $416 per day in products or services. These numbers represent what the business world calls KPIs or key performance indicators. These are predetermined goals with bench marks established that allow you to measure your progress. Now you can monitor your KPI daily, weekly and monthly to ensure you reach your intended goal. Monitoring is essential to the process so you will know how to adjust your work on a daily basis. If for some reason you are not hitting your goal, more than likely, it is in your IPAs or income producing activities.

One thing we know for sure is that numbers are reliable. When selling, there is a concept called The Rule of the Third. What's so amazing is throughout my sales career, when I hit my KPI or target number, I reached my goal. If I did not, the goal simply was not met.

For example: If your goal is 10 new customers per month, then your target should be 100 calls. Out of 100 calls to get the appointment, you should be able to schedule approximately 33 presentations. Keep in mind not all appointments will hold and will need to be rescheduled and some may change their minds. That's why it's very important to put follow up systems in place to increase the likelihood of the appointment holding.

So, if you have strong systems in place and optimally, you conduct 33 presentations, chances are you will achieve your goal of 10 new clients. However, the key is to make sure it's your ideal client and they fit within your target market. The stronger salesperson you become the greater your closing ratios will be but you must establish your KPI and work your numbers.

Exactly, what will you say when you are in front of your prospective client? Your presentation must be concise and you must be prepared to listen to your potential customer's needs and find their pain. Once you have identified their need, now it's time to provide them with the solution. You must be comfortable with your product or service, understand its feature and benefits well and be able to articulate them to your potential client in your presentation. Somewhere between listening and identifying their needs and you delivering the presentation, the relationship is secured.

Keep in mind, selling is also leveraging your brand in order to produce the desired outcome. You leverage your brand as you communicate the features and benefits of your product or service. Sharing the features and benefits is like painting a picture and having your client see themselves in it. Once they can see it, you have a sale.

Anthony Shipman, a business broker, shared five statements he gives prior to presentations. I found them to be very effective; hence, I created a modified version. Once the appointment has been scheduled, it's time to secure the relationship. In the initial conversation, uncover their needs and then share the following steps confidently before you present your services:

1. This is what I can do for you (The solution to their pain)

2. This is how I will go about it (Be sure it's aligned with their personality type, if not, you may lose them here)

3. This is how it will benefit you (Extremely important – this

paints them into the picture)

4. This is why I'm qualified to do it (Can increase trust factor)

5. The next step & give timeframe (Let's them know it's decision making time)

When you finish saying the fifth step, ask them, "Now, how does that sound?" It lets your prospective customer know you're not just telling but being inclusive. However, you are still in control of the direction of the conversation and the potential client will respect and appreciate your confidence.

Once they respond, which will undoubtedly be favorable, you can begin your presentation. Remember to speak to the pain in the beginning but then focus on the solution and benefits with your prospective customer. For example, a sales representative in a home furnishing store would welcome you, identify your needs and assume the sale by saying statements like, "This mattress is designed for people with lower back pain. Can you imagine getting a good night's rest and having less back pain when you sleep on your new mattress? You're going to begin feeling so much better!"

In these two questions, you have spoken to the issue, given the features and benefits and painted your new client into the picture. Now, he can see himself feeling better and can picture this mattress on his bed's frame.

Next is the closing question. Look your new client in his right eye, smile gently and ask, "So when would you like your mattress delivered? We have tomorrow or the following day available for delivery?" After asking the questions, tilt your head slightly but confidently and be very quiet. You have just assumed the sale, now it's time to close.

When closing the sale, be quick to listen for objections but be slow to respond. Remember, to reiterate the features and benefits, be authentic and continue painting your new client into the picture. Chances are you made the sale. If not, establish follow up because you have just built a new relationship. Either that person will buy now, later or refer his friends and family to you. Remember to ask for the referral.

There are many more techniques and tools to enhance your selling skills but if you utilize the techniques discussed you will build your confidence, your ratios will increase and you will become a confident salesperson. An excellent resource to enhance your skills is Brian Tracy's book, The Art of Closing the Sale.

The Winning Pitch

You have 30 seconds to make a good impression, give a great pitch, and leave feeling like you have attracted a new client. Preparation and confidence will determine the effectiveness of your delivery and the outcome of your connection.

An elevator pitch, elevator speech, or elevator statement is a short summary used to quickly and simply define a person, profession, product, service, organization or event and its value proposition. It is not a sales pitch but a clear and brief message or "commercial" about you which communicates who you are, what you're looking for and how you can benefit your potential client. Your goal is to leave them wanting to know more or remembering you when you follow up with a phone call.

You are on the elevator with a potential new client and you're going to the 5th floor. First of all, how is your image: clothes, hair, teeth, shoes, attitude, etc.? Do you feel confident and are you ready with your pitch, business cards and brochures?

You notice the lady has a beautiful handbag and is a very sharp dresser. Your company carries exclusive handbags and you just received a shipment with one-of-a-kind bags from France. You smile, greet the prospective client and compliment her on her handbag, now what? Remember, you only have 30 seconds and five floors to capture her attention, what do you say and what should you focus on? Below are a few suggestions. It should include 25 – 30 seconds of concise 8 – 10 sentences spoken with enthusiasm and passion. The 30 seconds should be power-packed with the following:

1. Introduction of yourself, your company and what you do with a hook that piques curiosity

2. Share problems solved with previous clients in a memorable example if time permits

3. Why you're sharing information with them

4. What sets you apart from the competition and how you work if time permits

5. A request or call to action

Example:

I'm Pamela Lue-Hing with Legacy Partners. So, you own your business? Our company shows small business owners how to connect their ideas to their dollars and grow their business with an action plan that works. Here's my card. I would like to learn more about the services you offer and see if there are any synergies. I am available tomorrow at 2 p.m. or 4 p.m. What time works best for you?

Always give specific days and times from which to choose. It works best when only two options are offered. This adds a sense of urgency and direction in scheduling. Follow the suggestions above and create your elevator pitch. The most important step is practicing in front of the mirror and then with a friend or family member several times before taking it to the elevator.

~Reflections~

Step #12

Plan Your Work and Work Your Plan

"For I know the plans I have for you," declares the Lord, "plans to prosper you and not to harm you, plans to give you hope and a future. Then you will call upon me and come and pray to me, and I will listen to you. You will seek me and find me when you seek me with all your heart.

~ Jeremiah 29:11-13 NIV~

Transfer Business Plan into Action Plan

Focus on the Targets

Ready, Aim, Fire!

Transfer Business Plan to Action Plan

Congratulations, you made it to Step #12! Developing and growing a business is so much like giving birth to a child. During the developmental stages of the unborn child, the parents experience a range of emotions. There's the anticipation of the new life, morning sickness, doubt if you will be good parents, preparation, and if it's your first, you spend countless hours studying about childbirth and parenthood.

Then the big day comes and there's excitement, fear and yes, tons of pain as you push that baby out and if you're daddy, you may be experiencing an extreme amount of stress, pain and discomfort as mom is squeezing your hand for dear life. All of the pains, stresses and discomfort are par for the course.

Now that you've created your business, you may be wondering if it can stand on its own two legs. The same way parents give life to a child, you have given life to your business by way of a "living document" called a business plan. You must move from being strategic to being tactical and plan the steps necessary to transfer your business plan into an action plan.

In your business plan, you have established your goals and set 3–5 year targets. Those targets should now be extracted and broken down into annual goals. A separate document will be required and should contain the following categories in a bullet point format:

- **Date Action Plan Created**

- **Mission Statement** (no bullets)
- **Business Goals**: Should be SMART – Specific, Measurable, Actionable and Agreed upon by all parties, Realistic, Timely and Trackable
- **Business Strategies and Objectives**
- **Total Yearly Budget with Income Projections and Explanation Cost Projection and Explanation**
- **Income Streams/Core Services**: A list of all products and services
- **Future Income Streams:** Future products or services to be launched
- **Expenses**: Office space, office supplies, licensure, etc.
- **Personal Achievements**: List all credentials, degrees, accomplishments
- **Personal Growth Goals**: Skills to improve and new credentials

This Action Plan is designed to further refine the targets so that they are more manageable and will serve as a springboard to create accountability. The plan should be reviewed quarterly and revised annual.

Focus on the Targets

After the action plan is complete, create a business model which reflects your core services or income streams. It should also contain the specific target audience or market, how you plan to market to them (reach them), what you plan to do when you connect with them and when you will make contact. This should be posted in your office so you can see it often.

Business Model

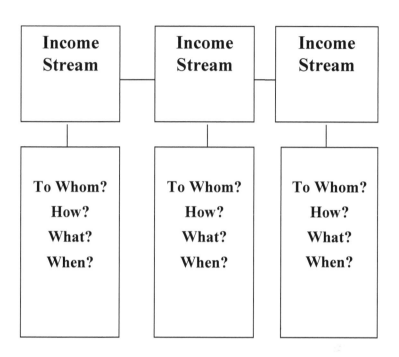

Based on the Action Plan and specifically the income projections, you will create a plan for each income stream/core service and what the goals will be quarterly, weekly and daily. This is the time to refer back to the sales information in Step #11 and determine your KPIs. Focusing on the targets is critical to the success of the Action Plan. There are 86,400 seconds in a day: Second by Second, Moment by Moment, Hour by Hour, Day by Day, Month by Month, Quarter by Quarter, Year by Year – Make the most of each period of time because if you don't, time will manage you and it will be increasingly difficult to stay on task.

Ready, Aim, Fire!

What is the difference between poor, good, great, and amazing outcomes? It's that challenging word called habits. Habits create patterns in our lives whether they are productive or counterproductive. These patterns are present in every area. So, if you find yourself in a pattern you are not pleased with, decide to create new habits which will change your patterns and create the discipline you need to impact your goals. Now is the time to adjust the sail, because the ship has left the dock and the captain must be on board.

In order to maximize your day, consider scheduling visionary moments daily to help create new habits or refine your patterns.

1. Time with God
2. Time with your vision
3. Time with your plan
4. Time to create action items

Now, imagine your ideal work day. Think about how you could structure your day to produce the results you want from your business and the lifestyle you desire. Write it down. After all, this is your business and your schedule is up to you. As you begin to create your calendar, be mindful that it takes carving out consistent blocks of time in all facets and activities of your life to build momentum.

As discussed in Step #10, systems drive the operations of a company and core functions drive the systems. Your core functions will become your daily action plan. At this point, all of your systems should be divided into the core functions: Marketing, Production, Administrative and Personal/ Professional Development (refer to example on page 158).

Marketing

- ☐ Social Media (FB, Twitter, Linked In)
- ☐ Prospective clients
- ☐ One on one prospective client meetings
- ☐ Networking event
- ☐ Speaking engagements (Workshops, Seminars, etc.)

Production

- ☐ Book Development
- ☐ Workshop Material Development
- ☐ Audio production
- ☐ Project Management for clients

Administrative

- ☐ Newsletters
- ☐ Current client follow up
- ☐ Emails
- ☐ Correspondence (letters, thank you notes)

Personal & Professional Development

- ☐ Spiritual/Family Time
- ☐ Exercise
- ☐ Educational Workshops

Make sure all of your systems have been placed under a Core Function. The next step is to create a color coded weekly plan sheet. Decide on the number of hours you will commit to your business and assign a color to each of the Core Functions. As you decide on the number of hours for each core function, take into consideration that Marketing and IPAs (income producing activities) should consume most of the day until your customer base increases.

Now determine the number of hours you will spend on each Core Function daily and place it on the calendar. You have just created a master calendar for your daily work which will help you remain accountable, ensure you're doing the right activities at the right time and you will be able to track the return on your investment of time.

Even when you can't see the progress, keep moving forward anyway and working your plan. Don't worry about things you can't control and use your weekly plan sheet to focus on the things you can control. Eventually, it will happen as long as your plan is effective and you are consistent.

In a post written on January 22, 2012, by Marc Chernoff in The Marc and Angel Hack Life: Practical Tips for Productive Living, he gave a summary of how successful people differentiate themselves. Twelve things successful people do differently are:

1. They create and pursue S.M.A.R.T. goals.
2. They take decisive and immediate action.
3. They focus on being productive, not being busy.

4. They make logical, informed decisions.

5. They avoid the trap of trying to make things perfect.

6. They work outside of their comfort zone.

7. They keep things simple.

8. They focus on making small continuous improvements.

9. They measure and track their progress.

10. They maintain a positive outlook and learn from their mistakes.

11. They spend time with the right people.

12. They maintain balance in their life.

~Reflections~

Author's Note

When Passion and Experience Unite

"The first step in the acquisition of wisdom is silence, the second
listening, the third memory, the fourth practice,
the fifth teaching others."
~ Solomon Ibn Gabriol ~

So it is, with the words of Solomon Ibn Gabriol, I've shared my knowledge. When I started my journey almost four years ago, I was exposed to countless business resources but it was as if they were a part of a one thousand piece puzzle. What I have found is it's a continuous cycle of putting pieces together as you move forward.

Ultimately, my goal is to help you break free of feeling like your destiny is determined by someone else and to give you the essential tools and information you need to develop and grow your company. This book was written to make your journey easier. It should serve as just one tool in your arsenal, as there is an unlimited amount of available resources.

For as long as I can remember, business has intrigued me and I have been surrounded by entrepreneurs. My entire life, especially the last several years has led to this very moment. I have been entrenched in studying, gathering resources and building my arsenal just for you, myself and others who take the risk and move out of their comfort zone.

Entrepreneurship is the cornerstone of this country. Indeed, it is not for those who are determined to stay in their comfort zones but for the few who dare to step out on faith and use their God-given talents to change a life and make an impact in our world. I told my story, now you can tell yours.

One of the most challenging tasks of entrepreneurship is not running the business but managing yourself. People tend to forget about the other important aspects of self like; spiritual growth, taking care of your health and well-being, and the importance of spending time with family. My prayer is that you will use this book to remind you to take care of you and to equip yourself with the ability to create a strong foundation on which to grow. You are the most important asset to your business so I challenge you not to just read the pages in this book, but put them into action.

If you embrace entrepreneurship, so many benefits await you like writing your own paycheck and giving yourself a raise when you want one. You have an opportunity to be your own boss; schedule your business around things that really matter to you like picking your children up from school instead of sending them to latchkey; taking care of an ailing parent, or playing golf during the middle of the day. You control with whom you work and have the capacity to create a legacy for those closest to you. The tax advantages are many but most important, you are investing your time versus spending your time on something that is not yours. Your business belongs to you!

One of the wisest decisions you can make as a business owner is to create a "Success Team." It will prevent you from reinventing the wheel, give you the resources and support you need, and give you the reason to persevere during the difficult days. You will make mistakes and I promise you I could write another book on mine. But remember those mustard seed opportunities are small moments in time that grow into great lessons to live by and pass on to future generations.

If you are stuck in the world of procrastination and telling yourself one day you will start your business and you've been saying it for the past 20 years now, today is your day! If you have been downsized and released to pursue your dreams, today is your day!

Perhaps you are already in business and have hit a brick wall, you've been arrested by self doubt and the negative thoughts are holding you hostage, remember the story of the donkey and the well, written by an unknown but skillful author.

One day a farmer's donkey fell down into a well. The animal cried piteously for hours as the farmer tried to figure out what to do. Finally, he decided the animal was old, and the well needed to be covered up anyway; it just wasn't worth it to retrieve the donkey.

He invited all his neighbors to come over and help him. They all grabbed a shovel and began to shovel dirt into the well. At first, the donkey realized what was happening and cried horribly. Then, to everyone's amazement he quieted down. A few shovel loads later, the farmer finally looked down into the well. He was astonished at what he saw. With each shovel of dirt that hit his back, the donkey was doing something amazing. He would shake it off and take a step up.

As the farmer's neighbors continued to shovel dirt on top of the animal, he would shake it off and take a step up. Pretty soon, everyone was amazed as the donkey stepped up over the edge of the well and happily trotted off!"

In life, you will find yourself in many wells. The key to getting out of the well is to shake it off and take a step up. Each of our challenges is a stair case to our destiny. We can get out of the deepest wells just by never giving up! Shake it off and take a step up.

As an entrepreneur, there will be days you fall into a place of darkness where light seemingly can not be found. It is during those times you should remember the donkey and the well story; do what the donkey did, shake it off and step up!

After I was downsized for the third time, I read a book that lit my soul on fire and set me in motion, The Shack by William Paul Young. He said "…if anything matters, then everything matters. Because you are important everything you do is important. Every time you forgive, the universe changes; every time you reach out and touch a heart or a life, the world changes; with every kindness and service, seen or unseen, my purposes are accomplished and nothing will ever be the same again."

Embrace your imperfections and don't get distracted by what others say. Remember, success is created in imperfection. You have been blessed with everything you need to do what you have been called to do. The world is waiting for you! Are you ready?

Your Partner in Success ~ Pamela

"I believe anything is possible. I see opportunity when others see impossibility. I take risks. I'm focused. I hustle. I know that nothing is unrealistic. I feel overwhelming love. I embrace my childlike wonder and curiosity. I take flying leaps into the unknown. I contribute to something bigger than myself. I create. I learn. I grow. I do. I believe it's never too late to start living a dream. I am an ENTREPRENEUR."

~ Author unknown ~

~ Peace and Blessings ~

References

Life Application Study Bible, New International Version

Bible, English Standard Version

The Chicken and the Eagle Story, posted by Gulf Breeze News, DjiXas 8/19/10

Dr. Mel Carbonnel, So, You're Unique! What's Your Point?

Michael E. Gerber, The E-Myth Revisited: Why Most Small Businesses Don't Work and What to Do About It

George Santayana, Reason in Common Sense, The Life of Reason, Volume 1

Jane Porter, 10 Questions to Ask Before Hiring a Tax Accountant Posted on m.entrepreneur.com 1/14/13

The Food and Agriculture Organization of the United Nations, Corporate Document Repository: Guidelines for Small-scale Fruit and Vegetable Processors

James Collins and Jerry Porras, Built to Last: Successful Habits of Visionary Companies

Laura Lakes, What is Branding and How Important is it to Your Marketing Strategy

Elyshia Brooks, Branding the Authentic You: Building a Conscious-Centered Brand & Lifestyle That Speaks To Your Extraordinary Self

Eker Millionaire Mind Intensive T. Harv Eker Signature Program: Marketing, Production, Administrative and Personal

www.experian.com/small-business/how-to-build-an-email-list.jsp

Anthony Shipman, Five Stages of Securing the Relationship

Brian Tracy's, The Art of Closing the Sale

Marc Chernoff, The Marc and Angel Hack Life: Practical Tips for Productive Living, 1/22/12

William Paul Young, The Shack

Website Sources

www.about.com

www.bplans.com

www.businessdictionary.com

www.businessknowhow.com

www.census.gov

www.charmeck.org

www.connect.ncdot.gov/business

www.dce.harvard.edu

www.doa.state.nc.us

www.dictionary.com

www.entrepreneur.com

www.experian.com

www.fao.org

www.forbes.com

www.google.com

www.marcandangel.com

www.mashable.com

www.investopedia.com

www.irs.gov

www.smallbusiness.chron.com

www.sba.gov

www.wikihow.com

www.wikipedia.com

Business Language and Terminology

Administrative
Of or relating to the running of a business, organization, etc.

Advertising or advertizing
In business is a form of marketing communication used to encourage or persuade an audience (viewers, readers, or listeners; sometimes in a specific group) to take or continue to take some action.

Business
Also known as an enterprise or a firm, is an organization involved in the trade of goods, services or both to consumers

Business Funnel
Sequence of Marketing, Sales, Finance, Operations, and Production

Business Plan
In its simplest form, a business plan is a guide – a roadmap for your business that outlines goals and details how you plan to achieve those goals.

C-Suite
A widely-used slang term used to collectively refer to a corporation's most important senior executives. C-Suite gets its name because top senior executives' titles tend to start with the letter *c*, for chief, as in chief executive officer, chief operating officer and chief information officer. Also called "C-level executives."

Chief Executive Officer
The Chief Executive Officer or CEO is generally, the most senior corporate officer (executive) or administrator in charge of managing a for-profit or non-profit organization. An individual appointed as CEO of a corporation, company, organization, or agency typically reports to the board of directors.

Chief Operating Officer

Also referred to as Director of Operations (or Operations Director) can be one of the highest-ranking executives in an organization and comprises of the "C-Suite." The COO is responsible for the daily operations of the company, and routinely reports to the highest ranking executive, usually the chief executive officer.

Competitive Research Analysis (Competitive Analysis)

In marketing and strategic management is an assessment of the strengths and weaknesses of current and potential competitors. It allows for effective and efficient strategy, formulation, implementation, monitoring and adjustment.

Corporation

A separate legal entity that has been incorporated either directly through legislation or through a registration process established by law. Incorporated entities have legal rights and liabilities that are distinct from their employees and shareholders, and may conduct business as either a for-profit or non-profit.

Customer Relations Management (CRM)

A system for managing a company's interactions with current and future customers. It involves using technology to organize, automate and synchronize sales, marketing, customer service, and technical support.

Customer Service

Is a provision of service to customers before, during and after a purchase. According to Turban et al (2002), "Customer service is a series of activities designed to enhance the level of customer satisfaction, the feeling that a product or service has met the customer expectation."

Elevator Pitch

A succinct and persuasive sales pitch or short summary used to quickly and simply define a person, profession, product, service, organization or event, and its value proposition.

Entrepreneurship

An individual who organizes or operates a business or businesses. In political economics, entrepreneurship is defined as the process of identifying and starting a new business venture and sourcing and organizing the required resources while taking both the risks and rewards associated with the venture.

Feasibility Study

An assessment of the practicality of a proposed plan or method.

Flowchart

A diagram of the sequence of movements or actions of people or things involved in a complex system or activity.

Human Resources

The personnel of a business or organization, especially when regarded as a significant asset. The department of a business or organization that deals with the hiring, administration, and training of personnel.

Key Performance Indicator (KPI)

Is a type of performance measurement. An organization may use KPIs to evaluate it success, or to evaluate the success of a particular activity in which it is engaged.

Limited Liability Corporation (LLC)

A limited liability company is a flexible form of enterprise that blends elements of partnership and corporate structures. An LLC is not a corporation; it is a legal form of company that provides limited liability to its owners in the vast majority of United States jurisdictions.

Marketing

The action or business of promoting and selling products or services, including market research and advertising.

Marketing Funnel

A structured method for developing products and/or service offerings at multiple price points, designed to entice prospects to first divulge their contact information, then make an initial purchase, followed by additional purchases.

Marketing Plan
A comprehensive blueprint which outlines an organization's overall marketing efforts.

Multi-level Marketing
A marketing strategy in which the sales force is compensated not only for sales they personally generate, but also for the sales of the other salespeople they recruit.

Networking
A socioeconomic business activity by which groups of like-minded business people recognize, create, or act upon business opportunities. The opportunity to build new business relationships and generate business at the same time.

Pipeline
The flow of potential clients which a company has started developing.

Production
The processes and methods used to transform tangible inputs (raw materials, semi-finished goods, sub-assemblies) and intangible inputs (ideas, information, knowledge) into goods or services.

Product Development
The creation of products with new or different characteristics that offer new or additional benefits to the customer. It may involve modification of an existing product or its presentation, or formulation of an entirely new product that satisfies a newly defined customer want or market niche.

Professional Development
Developing skills to strengthen a professional profile and increase knowledge to leverage opportunities.

Profit
A financial gain, especially the difference between the amount earned and the amount spent in buying, operating, or producing something.

Public Relations
The state of the relationship between the public and a company or other organization.

Publicity
The notice or attention given to someone or something by the media.

Quarter
A quarter refers to one-fourth of a year and is typically expressed as "Q." The four quarters that make up the year are: (Q1) January, February, and March; (Q2) April, May, and June; (Q3) July, August, and September; and (Q4) October, November and December.

Sales Funnel
In business science a sales process describes an approach to selling a product or service. The sales process has been approached from the point of view of an engineering discipline.

Strategic
Strategic thinking that involves the generation and application of unique business insights and opportunities intended to create competitive advantage for a firm or organization.

Strategic Planning
According to the Balanced Scorecard Institute, an organizational management activity that is used to set priorities, focus energy and resources, strengthen operations, ensure that employees and other stakeholders are working toward common goals, establish agreement around intended outcomes or results, assess and adjust the organization's direction accordingly.

Sole Proprietor
Someone who owns an unincorporated business by himself or herself.

SWOT Analysis
A study undertaken by an organization to identify its internal strengths and weaknesses, as well as, its external opportunities and threats.

Tactical
Of or pertaining to a maneuver or plan of action designed as an expedient toward gaining a desired end or temporary advantage.

Target Market
A group of customers towards which a business has decided to aim its marketing efforts and ultimately its merchandise. A well-defined target market is the first element to a marketing strategy.

United States Census Bureau
The United States Census Bureau (USCB), officially the Bureau of the Census, is a principal agency of the U.S. Federal Statistical System responsible for producing data about the American people and economy.

Value Proposition
A promise of value to be delivered and acknowledged and a belief from the customer that value will be appealed and experienced.

Funding Sources

Business Expansion Funding Corporation

www.befcor.com

BEFCOR, a company that helps you invest in your business and North Carolina's future by assisting you with 504 loans through the U.S. Small Business Administration. BEFCOR is a Charlotte-based 504 lender and helps businesses throughout the area to secure and manage their 504 loans. BEFCOR also has staff located in the triangle region of the state to better serve our customers.

Centralina Development Corporation

www.cdccapital.com

Centralina Development Corporation, Inc. (CDC), a non-profit corporation, was designated a Regional Certified Development Company by the U.S. Small Business Administration (SBA) in 1982. We finance small business enterprises with the SBA 504-Loan, which provides business owners in our region capital resources to finance real estate and fixed assets for growth and expansion, and job creation.

Self-Help Credit Union

www.self-help.org

The nonprofit Center for Community Self-Help (or Self-Help) combines several organizations that together provide financing, technical support, consumer financial services and advocacy for those left out of the economic mainstream. These entities include: Self-Help Credit Union, Self-Help Federal Credit Union, Self-Help Ventures Fund and the Center for Responsible Lending. In its 2013 Annual Report, Self-Help provided more than $168 million in financing to families, businesses and nonprofit.

U. S. Small Business Administration (SBA)

www.sba.gov

The Small Business Administration (SBA) is a United States government agency that provides entrepreneurs and small businesses a variety of assistance including loans, loan guarantees, counseling, training and workshops, bond guarantees and business advocacy.

Business Resources

Central Piedmont Community College

www.cpcc.edu.sbc

The Small Business Center at CPCC provides the local business community tuition-based courses, a non-degree certificate program, networking events, free seminars, no-cost counseling and a business resource library.

Charlotte Business Resources

www.charlottebusinessresources.com

A website designed to provide information and resources to business owners in the City of Charlotte and the surrounding business community.

Dun and Bradstreet Number

www.dnb.com

The Dun and Bradstreet DUNS (Data Universal Numbering System) is a worldwide method of classifying businesses. The number can be used to uniquely identify a business, or to link it to other entities within a corporation.

National Institute of Minority Economic Development

www.ncimed.org

NCIMED is a nonprofit consulting and services organization focused on creating business and economic success through diversity. NCIMED's Women's Business Center of North Carolina (WBC) helps women-owned businesses start and grow.

Service Corps of Retired Executives

www.charlotte.score.org

SCORE is a nonprofit association comprised of more than 13,000 volunteers dedicated to educating entrepreneurs and helping small businesses start, grow, and succeed nationwide. SCORE is a resource partner with the U.S. Small Business Administration (SBA), and has been mentoring small business owners for more than forty years. They offer small business entrepreneurs confidential business counseling services at no charge. The also offer workshops and other events.

Small Business and Technology Development Center

www.sbtdc.org

The SBTDC is a non-profit program of The University of North Carolina System that serves as a resource for growing and developing businesses. They also partner with the U.S. Small Business Administration.

Ventureprise, Inc.

www.venturprise.org

Ventureprise, Inc. (formerly The Ben Craig Center) is a regional public-private non-profit supports the success of start-up and early-stage entrepreneurs. Ventureprise accomplishes this through a program of education, networking, access to capital, and business incubation and acceleration services.

About the Author

Pamela is the founder and strategic consultant of Legacy Partners, LLC, a company that specializes in putting ideas into action. The company partners with small businesses to provide strategic coaching and consulting, sales development training, and manages special projects. The company also provides workshops, seminars, and professional facilitation services.

For the last 20 years, she has focused on developing people, programs and businesses. Pamela has extensive knowledge in strategic planning, thirty years in Sales and Marketing, and a wealth of knowledge as an enterprising entrepreneur. She draws upon her knowledge as a Board Certified Life Coach and Human Behavior Consultant to bring a "whole" new meaning to doing business.

She strongly believes in Luke 12:48, "To whom much is given, much is required." As such, she volunteers for the executive leadership team for the YBM Leadership Alliance program, moderates Mecklenburg County Commissioner Vilma D. Leake's bi-monthly Small Business Consortium meetings and serves on the Small Business and Entrepreneurship Advisory Board for Mecklenburg County, as well as, several ministries in her church.

As a keynote speaker, moderator, workshop and seminar facilitator, she connects with the audience and brings subject matter to life. Pamela is best known for her ingenuity in building something from nothing and her uncanny ability to see the big picture as well as the small details. Her "no non-sense, methodical, make-it-happen" style takes clients from where they are to where they want to be.

Pamela has a BA in Public Relations/Communication but her greatest accomplishments and joy in life are her son, Allonte' and daughter, Carrington.

~Notes~

~Notes~

Made in the USA
Charleston, SC
13 February 2015